BLUEPRINT FOR BAND

A GUIDE TO TEACHING COMPREHENSIVE MUSICIANSHIP THROUGH SCHOOL BAND PERFORMANCE

BY ROBERT GAROFALO, PH.D.

SCHOOL OF MUSIC

THE CATHOLIC UNIVERSITY OF AMERICA

WASHINGTON, D.C.

PUBLISHED BY MEREDITH MUSIC PUBLICATIONS

In Memory

of

John Paul

BLUEPRINT FOR BAND

CONTENTS

ISBN: 0-9624308-7-0

PREFACE

This book was written to provide school band directors with a curriculum guide for teaching comprehensive musicianship. Primary focus is on the concert band. The concert band is an ideal medium for teaching comprehensive musicianship, yet its rich potential for teaching about music beyond performance skills remains relatively undeveloped. In the approach suggested in this book, the inherent relationships that exist between music structure, style, and performance are consistently emphasized. Many suggestions are provided to help the band director correlate the teaching of musical concepts and skills through the performance repertoire.

The topics discussed in this book are those not commonly found in other publications of this type. These include comprehensive musicianship, aesthetic education, educational strategies, and instructional objectives. The ideas inherent in these topics are designed into a unified, yet flexible, curriculum model, or blueprint. The blueprint incorporates the latest research in the fields of education and music education, most notably the educational theories of Jerome Bruner of Harvard University, the Contemporary Music Project of the Music Educators National Conference, and the Hawaii Music Curriculum Project. In addition, the author has drawn upon his own personal research and many years of experience as a band director and music supervisor in designing the curriculum.

The first five chapters of this book present the proposed band curriculum in its entirety. Chapter One sets up the framework for organizing the curriculum, suggests the philosophical context and program content, and outlines the major components for teaching comprehensive musicianship: the unit study composition, the special study unit, band projects, and the source/reference notebook. Except for the source/ reference notebook, which is covered in Appendix A, these components are discussed in detail in the next four chapters. Chapter Two offers many practical suggestions for teaching comprehensive musicianship through a creative musical environment; band projects are included here along with several other teaching/ learning strategies. Chapter Three shows the director how to build a lesson plan for teaching comprehensive musicianship through a selected rehearsal/performance composition, the unit study composition. Chapter Four presents a complete model unit study composition based on Herbert Bielawa's *Spectrum* for prerecorded electronic tape and band. Chapter Five shows the director how to organize and teach the special study unit; four teaching models for this unit are presented.

The last chapter offers specific suggestions for implementing the curriculum in stages. These suggestions are intended to assist the band director in adopting or adapting the various curriculum components within the confines of an existing program. As band programs vary considerably from school to school, even within the same school district, it was necessary to design a high degree of flexibility into the proposed curriculum. Band directors whose programs are relatively small or developing should find this chapter helpful.

Although this book was written primarily for practicing band directors, others may find its contents of interest. School music supervisors and directors of music may wish to adopt various parts of the curriculum for use in their school systems. College and university teachers of instrumental music methods classes may wish to use this book as a text or for supplementary reading assignments. Finally, college band and wind ensemble directors may wish to use the model unit study composition as a basis for teaching comprehensive musicianship through their performing ensembles.

ACKNOWLEDGEMENTS

It is a pleasure to record here my gratitude to those who assisted me in the preparation of this book. To Doctors Spencer Cosmos and Michael Mark for their editorial assistance and many helpful suggestions, I am deeply grateful. A very special debt of gratitude is due Dr. Garwood Whaley and members of the Bishop Ireton—St. Mary's Symphonic Wind Ensemble for the opportunity to field-test several of the teaching models included in this book. Finally, thanks go to my wife and children for their patience and understanding, which remained constant throughout the two years that this book was in preparation.

Robert Garofalo
College Park, Maryland

PERSPECTIVE

Education in America is currently going through a revolutionary period of change. Recent developments have overwhelmed educators with a vast array of innovative ideas and a whole new vocabulary. Words like "accountability," "performance contracting," and "behavioral objectives" are gradually becoming familiar jargon among teachers. In addition, teachers are having to adjust to new modes of teaching and learning. Individualized instruction, team teaching, and differentiated staffing, for example, are creative approaches for meeting the needs of individuals involved in the educational process. They are, in large part, responses to some of the most highly criticized features of our educational system—its lack of individualization, the authoritarian role of the teacher, and rigid systems of grouping and grading. In the future, when these new educational ideas are widely adapted, refined, and assimilated, the result will be an improved quality of education in America.

Current Trends in Music Education

Current practices and trends in the field of music education have clearly been influenced by recent developments in education. Discussions of topical issues, such as instructional objectives, teaching/learning strategies, and flexible scheduling, have found their way into numerous music education journals and books. Music educators have also created their own unique approaches to teaching, such as comprehensive musicianship, aesthetic education, spiral curriculum, and so on. These latter approaches have grown out of a veritable boom in music education research and experimentation. The proliferation of government, university, and foundation-sponsored research is having a noticeable affect on the formation of new ideas about the why (philosophy), what (goals and objectives), and how (strategies) of music teaching. The Contemporary Music Project, Hawaii Music Curriculum Project, and Manhattanville Music Curriculum Program are a few of the research projects providing inspiration and guidance.

The Music Educators National Conference is also at the forefront of new directions in music education. For more than half a century MENC has been a guiding light for the profession. Through its many services and publications, MENC has sought to keep music educators enlightened and informed. In recent years, this organization has become a major catalyst for qualitative changes in music education. Task force study groups have been organized to re-evaluate everything from the goals and objectives of music education to the training of teachers. MENC's influence on the profession is pervasive and ongoing.

The effects of research and experimentation in music education can be seen in a number of progressive school music programs throughout the country. Secondary schools located in large metropolitan areas, for example, are likely to offer courses in music theory, history, and the humanities as a regular part of the curriculum in addition to band, orchestra, and chorus. Some secondary schools offer class piano, guitar, conducting, and private lessons as regularly scheduled, credited courses. There seems to be a minor trend toward offering a wider variety of music courses to a broader group of students.

To gain a true perspective on music education in the secondary schools today, one must examine the dominant role of the performing ensemble in the school curriculum. The American School Band Directors' Association has estimated that less than 20% of the nation's high school students participate in performing ensembles; the other 80% have little or no involvement in school music activities. At the junior high school level, the situation is noticeably different because general music is usually required for all students. Overall, however, there is a definite diminishing involvement in school music activities by students as they progress from seventh through twelfth grade.

The performing ensemble is an established part of most secondary school programs in America. Current practices and procedures of instrumental and vocal teachers are generally consistent throughout the United States and are firmly rooted in tradition. The tradition is strongly performance-oriented, highly competitive, and nonacademic, that is, lacking in curriculum content and structure. This has placed undue emphasis on the development of performance skills (technique), the weeding out of those who do not measure up to the competition (high level of selectivity), and the continued nonrecognition of music as a legitimate course of study on a par with other curriculum subjects, such as English, science, mathematics, and social studies. While these practices and procedures have served a useful purpose in the past, their continued use without modification is doubtful.

School Band Performance in the United States—Issues and Dilemmas

The current state of school band performance in the United States is accurately reflected in a major research study completed a few years ago by R. Jack Mercer.[1] Mercer spent four and a half months traveling the length and breadth of continental United States (17,567 miles) to interview 222 selected high school band directors. Two matched groups of band directors were interviewed, a nominated group of outstanding directors as rated by university judges, and a matched group of less outstanding band directors; both groups represented large and small schools. Because of the nature, scope, and validity of this study, its findings are of great significance; they underscore critical issues and dilemmas of instrumental music education in America.

Mercer discovered that most high school band programs suffer from "performancitis" (an average of 15.4 large group performances per year[2]); most scores are selected by "happenstance" (the needs of the next performance); and most band directors have no clear conception of what a band curriculum is, nor can they explain what they are trying to accomplish educationally with their students. Mercer originally intended to ask each director to describe his course of study or band curriculum. After the first fifty interviews, the question was dropped because the responses were almost identical; the directors interpreted the question to mean: "What rehearsal techniques do you use?"[3] Mercer concludes that band directors have been preoccupied with preparations for the next performance and have not taken time to develop comprehensive music curriculums:

> There are few carefully planned courses of study designed to teach students the fundamentals of music theory, introduce them systematically to the great composers, or assist them in comprehending the fascinating metamorphosis of musical form and style through the broad sweep of man's history. Instead, our students concentrate on acquiring the technical competence necessary to play the scores which we decide will make an interesting program for our next audience or will please our colleagues who will be judging the next contest.[4]

If Mercer's findings reflect the status quo of a majority of school band programs in the United States, the music education profession is in need of effective curriculum designs applicable to secondary school band programs.

From the growing body of research available today, a picture is beginning to emerge: band programs that place undue emphasis on performance and the development of performance skills are likely to be seriously deficient in teaching students about music. In summarizing the findings of several research studies, Charles Benner wrote:

It can be inferred that performing group participation has little effect on musical behavior other than the acquisition of performance skills, unless there is a planned effort by the teacher to enrich the performing experience with additional kinds of musical understanding.[5]

Research findings of the Manhattanville Music Curriculum Program seem to support the same conclusion: "Skill development does not necessarily lead to musical insight. . . . Performance *alone* [author's italics] is a relatively unreliable means for the nurturing of musical insight."[6] The need, then, stems not from the demand for more highly skilled performers and performances, but rather from a need for educationally sound curriculums that deal effectively with real learning about music.

There are many difficulties involved in designing band curriculums. Consider, for example:

—the philosophical problems that need to be resolved—problems that result from conflicting philosophies of education and music education, diverse theories of aesthetics and aesthetic education, and an infinite variety of personal beliefs on the part of band directors concerning the role of the performing ensemble in music education;

—the enormous problem of developing program objectives that can easily be translated into practical instructional objectives and stated in behavioral terms, and the related problem of developing means for evaluation;

—the difficulties involved in developing curriculum materials and providing adequate learning environments, such as listening facilities and source reading libraries;

—the problem of integrating and coordinating the band curriculum with other course offerings in music, such as theory, history, appreciation, and humanities, that may vary from school to school even within the same school system;

—the difficulties involved in setting up and coordinating a task force of experts—master teachers, supervisors, university professors, professional consultants—to develop, test, and evaluate new curriculum designs.

This representative list of problems may partially explain why there are relatively few effective band curriculums in use today. Band directors need not be discouraged, however, because interest in the subject is increasing and basic research is being carried out on several fronts at an accelerating pace.

For the performing ensemble director who is searching for a more effective and meaningful way to teach music, comprehensive musicianship through band performance may be the answer. Band directors who use this approach may have to modify their philosophies, redefine their goals and objectives, and reorganize their teaching strategies—in short, develop a comprehensive musicianship curriculum. The following chapters of this book were written as a guide to assist band directors in accomplishing this important task.

Footnotes

[1] For a detailed report on the findings of this monumental study, see R. Jack Mercer, *The Band Director's Brain Bank* (Evanston, Illinois: The Instrumentalist Company, 1970).

[2] The typical high school band director gives an average of 1.5 large group performances a month during the school year— one every two and one-half weeks! In addition, he prepares 13.2 ensembles for competition and coaches 21.5 soloists for contests each year. Mercer, pp. 13, 19.

[3] *Ibid.* p. 84.

[4] *Ibid.* Mercer found that approximately 50% of the high school bands participated in marching band contests, and over 75% participated in concert band festivals and competitions.

[5] Charles H. Benner, *Teaching Performing Groups: From Research to the Music Classroom No. 2* (Washington, D.C.: Music Educators National Conference, 1972), p. 10.

[6] Ronald B. Thomas, *MMCP Synthesis: A Structure for Music Education* (Elnora, New York: Media, Inc., 1971).

CHAPTER ONE

THE FRAMEWORK

The teaching of comprehensive musicianship through band performance may be defined as an all-inclusive, multifaceted approach to developing student musicianship. Musicianship here means one's knowledge and understanding of the creative and expressive qualities of music as revealed through the application of musical skills. In this approach, the band director's major responsibilities are twofold: (1) to organize a viable program of studies that correlates instrumental music performance with the study of music structure and style and encompasses a diversity of musical behaviors: performing, listening, analyzing, composing, conducting, arranging; and, (2) to establish a stimulating musical environment in which students are continually brought into contact with the "creative musical experience," either directly or indirectly.

This chapter provides a framework for organizing a comprehensive musicianship curriculum; the following chapters offer practical suggestions for teaching comprehensive musicianship through a creative musical environment.

The Content and Context

Before a band director can begin to teach comprehensive musicianship, he needs to have a clear conception of the content and context of his teaching. The program content is suggested in the Blueprint of Objectives given in Figure 1. The philosophical and practical framework for the blueprint is based on the understanding that the primary function of the performing ensemble is the learning of music within the context of aesthetic education. In this context, instrumental performance is not an end in itself, but a means to an end. That end includes the augmentation of knowledge and understanding of the structural elements of music and of music as a creative art form of man in a historical context; the cultivation of habits, attitudes, and appreciations; and, most important, the development of each student's aesthetic potential, his sensitivity and responsiveness to that which is beautiful in music. Although aesthetic sensitivity cannot be taught, it can be fostered through the use of educational strategies that involve analytical, judicial, and creative thinking. Through analysis, the student attempts to discover the true nature and inner relationships of the music he is performing. By using his judicial faculties, he makes value judgments concerning the quality and worth of the music. Utilization of both thinking processes helps the student to create music intelligently

Figure 1

Blueprint of Objectives

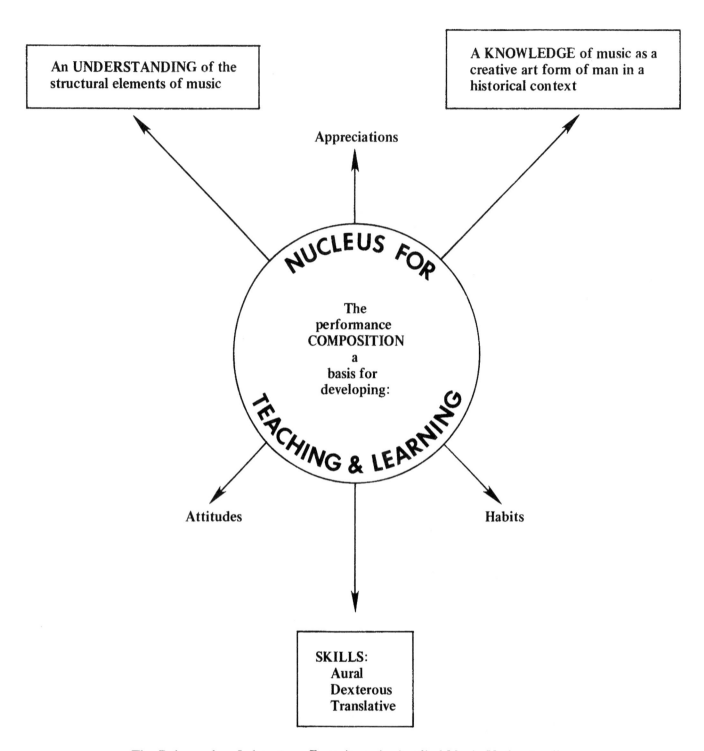

An UNDERSTANDING of the structural elements of music

A KNOWLEDGE of music as a creative art form of man in a historical context

Appreciations

NUCLEUS FOR

The performance COMPOSITION a basis for developing:

TEACHING & LEARNING

Attitudes

Habits

SKILLS:
Aural
Dexterous
Translative

The Rehearsal—a Laboratory Experience in Applied Music Understanding through performance. Practical application and development of these goals take place in the rehearsal hall. Therefore, the rehearsal should become a laboratory experience in applied music understanding, where both the formal structures and expressive qualities of the music being performed undergo analysis and where criteria for making value judgments are analyzed.[1]

The comprehensive musicianship curriculum suggested here is based on a carefully conceived Blueprint of Objectives. These program objectives are intended to give explicit direction to the total band curriculum. They are comprehensive in scope, yet flexible enough to be adapted to most school band programs.

In the blueprint shown in Figure 1, the score provides the nucleus from which all program objectives grow. Consequently, the selection of a qualitative repertoire is of critical importance in overall planning. Scores must be carefully selected and evaluated in terms of their teaching/learning potential, as measured against the blueprint, and not by "happenstance." The philosophic framework and Blueprint of Objectives provide the yardstick for the selection of the repertoire.

Important aspects of the Blueprint are outlined as follows:

I. *Understanding* of the structural elements of music
    A.   pitch
        1.   melody (horizontally organized pitches)
        2.   harmony (vertically organized pitches)
    B.   duration (rhythm)
    C.   timbre (individual or combined tone colors—bandstration)
    D.   intensity (dynamics)
    E.   texture (homophonic, polyphonic, and so on)
    F.   design (form)
    G.   compositional techniques and considerations
        1.   melodic (thematic) transformation
        2.   harmonic transformation (such as modulation)
        3.   rhythmic transformation
        4.   unity and variety (contrast)
        5.   dissonance and consonance (tension and relaxation)

II. *Knowledge* of music as a creative art form of man in a historical context
    A.   historical background information about a composition
    B.   biographical information about the composer
    C.   stylistic and performance practices of the historical period that the composition represents

III. *Skills*
    A.   aural skills (ear-oriented)
        1.   identification and discrimination of the structural elements of music (see under I, A to E)
            a.   pitches (including intonation)
            b.   durations (including ensemble, that is, rhythmic precision)
            c.   timbres (including tone quality and blend)
            d.   intensities (including balance)
            e.   textures
        2.   recognition tasks associated with extended listening (see under I, F and G)

B. dexterous skills (hand-oriented)
    1. instrumental
    2. conducting
    3. vocal (optional)

C. translative skills (eye-oriented)
    1. music reading
        a. individual parts
        b. multiple parts (score reading)
    2. sight reading

All six objectives of the blueprint are related in some way to established behavioral categories. The primary objectives, understanding, knowledge, and skills, focus on the development of concepts (cognitive domain) and skills (psychomotor domain). Attitudes, habits, and appreciations (affective domain) appear in the blueprint as important byproducts or outcomes of a process of education that deals effectively with the development of concepts and skills. They are developed by the individual bandsman from his personal assessment, made consciously or subconsciously, of the worth and quality of his own experiences with music. A list of outcomes should include the following: *attitudes*—(1) respect for the musical tastes of others, (2) positive feelings toward music and confidence in one's own creative potential, (3) desire to improve one's competence with music; *habits*—(1) preference for listening to quality music, (2) performance of music for enjoyment, either individually, or as a member of a group; *appreciations*—(1) responsiveness to the expressive and creative qualities in music, (2) discrimination of different styles and idioms of music, and (3) sensitivity to skilled and tasteful performance in music. These representative outcomes are really the ultimate goals of a comprehensive musicianship curriculum. The idea is to foster lasting musical attitudes, habits, and appreciations that will provide each student with a lifelong source of pleasure and enrichment.

Program objectives are meaningless statements, unless they are translated into specific instructional objectives, implemented on a daily basis through the use of teaching/learning strategies, and evaluated. The whole process is covered in detail in subsequent chapters. What follows is an overview of the proposed curriculum.

Overview of the Proposed Curriculum

To be valid, a band curriculum must have continuity, as well as content and a means of evaluation. The concerned band director may ask, "How do I organize my curriculum so that it is both developmental, that is has continuity and is not fragmented, and cyclical in design?" Knowledgeable writers on the subject have suggested a three- or four-year cycle of instruction to provide long-range continuity to the band curriculum. Joseph Labuta[2], for example, suggests a three-year sequence encompassing timbre and the materials of music, forms and styles of music, and interpretation and discrimination of music; in a four-year cycle, forms and styles of music would be separated. Other authorities have suggested similar types of cyclical sequences emphasizing slightly different content: music theory, history of music, appreciation, conducting, arranging, and so on. Organizing the curriculum into cycles of instruction merits careful consideration because it can provide some degree of continuity. The problem with this organizational pattern, however, is that it tends to segregate music and music instruction into separate parts, thus negating, to a certain degree, the whole idea of comprehensive musicianship. In the proposed curriculum, yearly cycles of instruction are incorporated, but only as supplementary instructional units called "special study units." The primary instructional unit, the unit study composition, is at the core of the curriculum; this mode of instruction is continuous, noncyclical, and represents a spiral organizational pattern. Although both units of instruction provide continuity to the curriculum, the unit study composition is more important because it is designed to integrate the development of concepts and skills.

The three major components in the proposed curriculum are: (1) instructional units, the unit study composition and the special study unit, (2) band projects, and (3) the source/reference notebook (see Figure 2). Instructional units constitute the major elements of which the band curriculum is made. An organized sequence of units constitutes the course of study for the band. An instructional unit may require a few days to complete or a few weeks, depending on the subject matter and type. Of the two types suggested, the unit study composition will take longer to complete because it is more comprehensive in scope.

The Unit Study Composition: The unit study composition is the *primary* instructional vehicle for teaching comprehensive musicianship in the curriculum. It is used to provide a structured introduction to basic musical concepts related to the structural elements of music: melody, harmony, rhythm, bandstration, dynamics, texture, and form (Blueprint of Objectives, Category I), and the historical context of music (Blueprint of Objectives, Category II). This conceptual framework is consistent with the "common-elements" approach suggested by the Contemporary Music Project of MENC:

A. Music consists of Sound, divisible into
   1. Pitch
      a. horizontal (melody)
      b. vertical (harmony)
   2. Duration (rhythm)
   3. Quality
      a. timbre
      b. dynamics
      c. texture

B. These sound elements are used to articulate shape, or *form* (including the possibility of lack of established form).
C. Every musical work must be viewed in its *context,* including stylistic, historical, cultural, and other considerations.[3]

The materials of the unit study composition include analytical and historical notes; glossary of musical terms; list of concepts, subconcepts, and behavioral objectives; activities and assignments with options; and a means for evaluation. These materials are developed into a lesson plan for the director and a study guide for the students. Detailed instructions on the construction and use of the unit study composition are given in Chapter Three. Chapter Four presents a complete unit study composition, a model lesson plan.

The Special Study Unit: The special study unit is a *supplementary* instructional unit used to cover a wide range of band-related topics; these topics may be concept-oriented, skill-oriented, or both. The instructional materials for this unit will, for the most part, take the form of student learning guides similar to those given in Chapter Five of this book. The format of the learning guide is as follows: rationale (a statement explaining why the subject should be taught/learned); behaviorally stated instructional objectives; activities, resources, and assignments with options; and a description of the method of evaluation to

6

Figure 2

Organizational Chart of the Proposed Band Curriculum

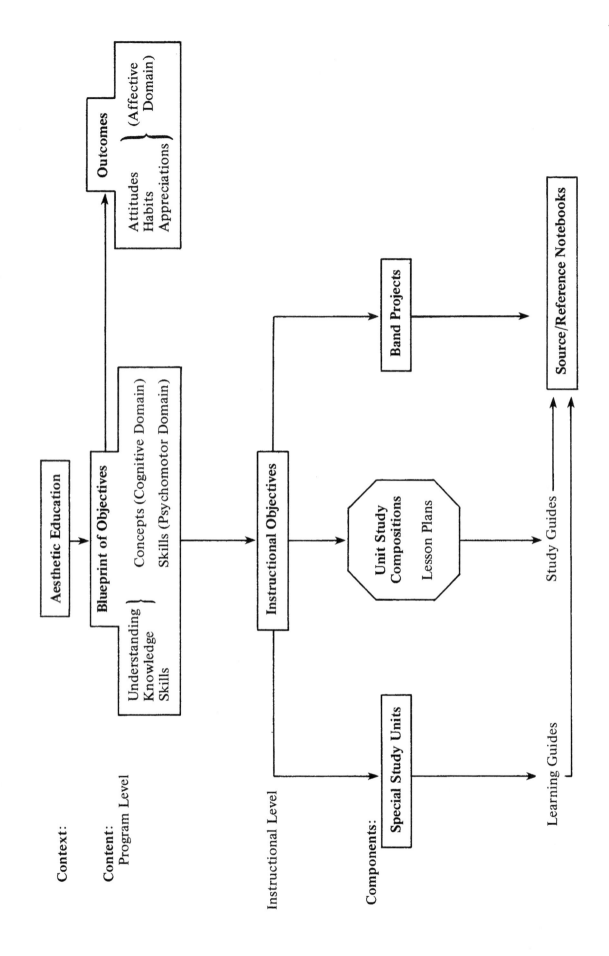

be used. Here is a partial list of suitable topics that can be taught through the special study unit:

1. Basic Conducting
2. Transposition and Scoring
3. Acoustics, Tuning, and Intonation
4. Sight Reading
5. Fundamentals of Music
6. Common Musical Terms
7. Instrument Care and Maintenance

These topics are covered in Chapter Five.

Band Projects: Band projects encompass a whole range of individualized learning activities. In the proposed curriculum, they are used to provide students with additional opportunities and outlets to meet their varying interests and abilities. The subject is covered in great detail in the next chapter.

The Source/Reference Notebook: The source/reference notebook is an important teaching/learning tool in the suggested curriculum; its use is highly recommended. Upon entering the program for the first time, the novice bandsman is given a basic notebook, an expanded version of the traditional program handbook (see Appendix A for the suggested format and content outline). Each year the student expands his notebook by adding all distributed and accumulated band materials: learning guides, study guides, band projects, reading and discussion notes, completed assignments, tests, and so on. The notebook is maintained by the student until he graduates from the school or permanently leaves the program. At that time, he is allowed to take his notebook with him. Periodic evaluations of the notebooks will insure that they are kept neat and up-to-date.

Although some components of the proposed curriculum have to be established in stages, others can be incorporated into existing programs almost immediately. The source/reference notebook, for example, can be written and assembled over the summer vacation and made ready for distribution to students when school begins in the fall. Once in use, the notebook can easily be revised and augmented as the curriculum evolves. Band projects can also be incorporated into existing programs with little or no trouble at all. All the band director has to do is compile a list of acceptable projects with guidelines and distribute the list to students along with the notebooks. If band projects are required twice a year, they can be turned in with the notebooks for evaluation.

Instructional units have to be incorporated gradually into the band program because it takes time to write materials for these units. In addition, the use of instructional units in the curriculum requires a change in the band director's modus operandi. Of the two instructional units discussed above, the special study unit is easier to organize and should be established first. Most band directors should be able to write learning guides for these units, using models provided in this book.

Unquestionably, the most difficult task involved in establishing the proposed curriculum is that of assembling a core of unit study compositions complete with historical and analytical notes, lesson plans, and student study guides. Although several instructional units of this type have already been published,[4] many more will be needed before a three- or four-year rotating repertoire of unit study compositions can be established. To facilitate the matter, it is highly recommended that a local committee of band directors be organized to prepare unit study materials based on a carefully selected and agreed-upon performance repertoire. The committee, a curriculum development task force, should include an instrumental music supervisor and a university music curriculum specialist as a consultant. Working together for a year or two, this group could develop a core of unit study compositions for use by all band directors in a school system.

To insure that all components of the curriculum are sequenced properly and functioning in harmony with each other, it is advisable to plan each year's work ahead of time. For example, the school year could be divided into time frames paralleling established evaluation periods. Known performance requirements for the year would be identified and blocked out in each time frame. At least one qualitative work would be selected from the repertoire scheduled for performance within each time frame and developed into a study units and a band project. This organizational plan would not only guarantee continuity, but it would also provide an objective basis for evaluating student growth for each grading period.

It is appropriate here to summarize, and thereby emphasize, important features of the proposed band curriculum:

—Instrumental music performance is viewed in the philosophical context of aesthetic education. In this context, music is recognized as a fine art subject in the total school curriculum to be taught/studied in and for itself. In band, emphasis is placed on developing in-depth "aesthetic experiences" through the performance and study of music

—The band curriculum is planned, organized, implemented, and evaluated on the basis of clearly stated objectives operational at two levels, program level and instructional level.

—The unit study composition is the primary instructional component in the curriculum. Through it, the inherent relationship that exists between music structure, style, and performance is emphasized. This relationship is revealed through a structured introduction of basic musical concepts, a "common-elements" approach. The rehearsal becomes a laboratory experience in applied music understanding.

—The band curriculum utilizes a variety of educational strategies, organizational and teaching/learning, to create a stimulating musical environment and to provide varied and flexible music experiences geared to meet the diverse needs of band students.

The teaching of comprehensive musicianship through school band performance is more than just an organized curriculum and Blueprint of Objectives; it is a process of education that focuses on the individual learner. In this approach, the band director's conception of the student's role in the process is critically important. He must recognize that the individual bandsman is more important than the group he plays in. In other words, the band must exist as a vehicle for nurturing the musical growth of the student and not the other way around. This leads to a consideration of the role of the band director in teaching comprehensive musicianship.

Role of the Band Director

Successful development of a viable comprehensive musicianship program depends almost entirely on the capabilities and attitude of the band director. What he does and how he does it reveals his concept or viewpoint of what instrumental music teaching is all about. If he views himself as a conductor, he may spend most of his time drilling students in rehearsals and conducting polished performances to build his reputation and satisfy his ego. If he views himself as a public relations man and crowd pleaser, he may put his efforts into developing a spectacular marching band. These typical viewpoints, while obviously a part of the overall picture, are too restrictive to be totally compatible with an aesthetically-oriented band program. A more acceptable viewpoint would be for the band director to consider himself first and foremost a "musician-educator." A clear concept of what a "musician-educator" is should help the band director to understand his role and to identify his strengths and weaknesses; self-analysis is a necessary first step to becoming an outstanding teacher.

To teach comprehensive musicianship, a band director has to be a comprehensive musician. A "musician" is usually thought of as one who is skilled in music, a competent performer. In a broader sense, with regard to music teaching, a "musician" is one who has total command of his subject matter, music. In addition to being competent in the skills of music (aural, dexterous, and translative), the band director needs to have an intelligent understanding of the theoretical and creative aspects of music organization and structure: composition, orchestration, form and analysis, counterpoint, theory, and so on; a broad knowledge of music history, style, and literature; and the ability to relate and interpret his understanding and knowledge in an aesthetically sensitive way through analysis and performance.

An "educator," from the Latin *educatus,* is one who develops and cultivates another's mental, moral, and aesthetic faculties. In a narrow sense, to educate also means to teach by imparting knowledge and giving information. This concept is out-of-tune with current educational thought. In the best sense of the word, to educate means to educe, from the Latin *educere*—to bring forth, and it implies drawing out of a person something potential or latent. This concept is consistent with a comprehensive musicianship curriculum that is student-centered rather than teacher-centered.

Obviously, if a band director wishes to educate someone else according to this latter definition, certain requisite knowledge and skills are necessary. First, he must know and understand his students—how they think, what they know and can do, what motivates them, what their likes and dislikes are, in short, all psychological and behavioral factors relating to their growth and development. Second, he must know how to teach—skills and techniques are necessary if one is to have an impact on student learning. If a band director is a musician and not an educator, or vice versa, the success of his program will be diminished in proportion to his deficiencies.

Music teaching is a demanding occupation. Since it is impossible to know all that one needs to know, it is incumbent upon the band director to continue to learn about music; teaching is a lifelong learning experience, "a process of becoming." Here is a basic rule of action: if you don't know something and you need to know it to be an effective teacher of comprehensive musicianship, study it privately, in a class, or on your own; whenever possible, relate what you are doing as a learner to what you are doing as a teacher. By following this rule, you will bring the excitement of your learning experiences into the rehearsal hall and thereby enhance the motivational aspects of your teaching.

Footnotes (Chapter One)

[1] Abraham Schwadron, *Aesthetic Dimensions for Music Education* (Washington, D.C.: Music Educators National Conference, 1967), p. 79.

[2] Joseph A. Labuta, *Teaching Musicianship in the High School Band* (West Nyack, New York: Parker Publishing Company, Inc., 1972), p. 24.

[3] *Comprehensive Musicianship: An Anthology of Evolving Thought* (CMP$_5$) (Washington, D.C.: Music Educators National Conference, 1971), p. 100.

[4] See Appendix B under Comprehensive Musicianship Source Materials.

CHAPTER TWO

SUCCESSFUL STRATEGIES FOR TEACHING COMPREHENSIVE MUSICIANSHIP

The techniques used by the band director to teach comprehensive musicianship on a day-to-day basis may be defined as teaching/learning strategies. A comprehensive list of strategies is given in Figure 3. All strategies listed need not be used for every instructional unit under study, nor is it necessary to require all students to complete any specific strategy at any given time. Certain strategies, such as band projects, work best if they are ongoing options.

Figure 3

Teaching/Learning Strategies

1. Listening and Reading Assignments
2. Projects in Creativity
3. Band Projects
4. Conducting Assignments
5. Group Discussions, Demonstrations, and Short Lectures
6. Chamber Music Performance and Study Activities
7. Field Trips
8. Guest Musicians
9. Concert and Lecture Series
10. Workshops, Clinics, and Festivals
11. Miscellaneous Strategies

Organizational Strategies

Educational strategies are of practical use only if there are adequate teaching/learning environments: source reading libraries, listening facilities, and so on.[1] Although a few band directors are ingenious at accomplishing a great deal under the most severe handicaps, there is no question that the effectiveness of a comprehensive musicianship curriculum is directly related to the quality of the environment within which it operates. Band directors should work diligently toward establishing these environments if they are not already available.

Source Reading Library: The task of building and maintaining a source reading library is not difficult.[2] You can start by enlisting the aid of the school librarian to help you expand the music holdings in the school library with existing library funds. Of course, you will have to provide a list of materials to be purchased. The list should include music reference books, dictionaries, and periodicals; books on the history of music, musical performance, and style; biographies of musicians; practical books on conducting, composing, arranging, and scoring; books on theory, form and analysis, counterpoint, acoustics, instrumental technique, care and maintenance of instruments, and the history of musical instruments. It is impractical to list here all of the items that should be included in a basic source reference library.[3] Furthermore, it is important for each band director to compile his own list so that the materials are relevant to his own developing curriculum.

Listening Facility: The establishment of a listening facility complete with turntables, tape decks, multiple earphone headsets, records, tapes, and scores should be given top priority by the band director. Again, the school library may be the appropriate place to begin. If possible, however, this facility should be located near the rehearsal hall. One band director who was highly respected for the quality of his program enlisted the aid of his parent booster association to raise $1,000 for the purpose of purchasing equipment for a music listening facility. After securing the funds, he converted a medium-sized storage room located near the rehearsal hall into a music listening and study facility. Within a few years, he was able to build a substantial collection of records, scores, and tapes with a minimal yearly budget allotment. Once a listening facility has been established, it is a relatively simple process to build the collection.[4] This can be done once a year at the same time that you are ordering performance music for your ensemble.

The Rehearsal Hall: If the rehearsal is to become a laboratory experience in applied music understanding, the rehearsal hall must be equipped like a laboratory with a variety of instructional hardware. The band director must not only secure this hardware if it is not already available, but he must also learn how to use the equipment effectively for instructional purposes. Basic tools include a quality tape recorder, stereo record player, piano, and electronic tuning devices; these should be used regularly to illustrate, demonstrate, and evaluate music and musical performance. Projectors and other audiovisual equipment, such as the videotape recorder, are also useful teaching/learning tools. The opaque and overhead projectors, for example, can be used in the rehearsal hall to teach musical concepts through the study of prepared musical examples and scores. The opaque projector requires little or no preparation of materials; score passages can be shown directly on the screen. With the overhead projector, however, some preparation of materials is needed in the form of transparencies. The videotape recorder can be used to tape student conductors, master classes, guest clinicians and performing groups, and noncopyrighted films. If your school has this equipment, take the time to find out how to use it for instructional purposes. The time-consuming task of setting up and using this equipment can be simplified by enlisting the aid of several interested and capable students. Work of this type is satisfying to young people.

Flexible Scheduling: The organization of a comprehensive musicianship curriculum requires a flexible approach to scheduling. Bringing flexibility into an established schedule represents a major challenge for the band director and may require a change in his attitude as well as alterations in his use of time. Of the various elements that one needs to consider in organizing a schedule, facilities, time, staff, students, and so on, time is probably the most important. In most cases, however, the problem is not one of finding more time in the schedule, as students already spend inordinate amounts of time in band;[5] rather, it is one of learning how to utilize time already available in a flexible and more efficient way. A number of suggestions are given intermittently throughout this book to aid the band director in organizing a flexible schedule. The following suggestions, therefore, are offered to supplement those already given.

One of the knottiest problems the band director has to solve in dealing with large performing groups is that of providing for individual differences and abilities. Within the framework of a traditional schedule, there are a number of flexible arrangements that can be used to challenge and motivate talented performers, and, at the same time, to allow for more intensive work with students of lesser abilities. Here are a few suggestions: (1) Encourage your first chair players to organize themselves into ongoing chamber music groups—trios, quartets, quintets. Help them get started by providing suitable literature, a place to rehearse, classroom, instrument storage room, office, almost any place will do, and a goal (a chance to perform in public). (2) Allow multitalented students the possibility of singing in the chorus or playing a string instrument in the orchestra by letting them divide their time between groups, if the large performing ensembles are scheduled at the same time. (3) Provide academically talented students with the opportunity to learn about music independently through the use of self-instructional materials, programmed theory workbooks, learning activity packets, instructional tapes and recordings, and so on.[6] These suggestions are representative of a number of possibilities open to the unselfish band director who is willing to excuse some of his best performers from one or two rehearsal periods each week.

The recurring fear expressed by many band directors that the performance level of their groups would drop, if they spent part of their rehearsal time teaching anything else but performance skills, seems unfounded. In fact, a growing number of published reports indicate that both concepts and skills can be taught through the performing ensemble by using innovative scheduling arrangements, and the performance levels can be raised rather than lowered.[7] The key factor in most innovative scheduling practices is flexibility. By providing students with varied opportunities to perform and study music in large groups, small groups, and independently, individual differences and needs are more likely to be taken care of. A few case studies of innovative scheduling practices currently in use will serve to illustrate the diversity and flexibility of those practices.

> *Band Program 1:* large suburban high school. Symphonic band is scheduled during lunch period. The school has three one-half hour lunch periods each day. Flexibility is automatically built into this schedule. On any given day, the band director can schedule the entire ensemble for an hour and twenty minutes of rehearsal time (allowing only ten minutes for lunch), call for sectional rehearsals back to back (one-half hour each for brass, woodwinds, and percussion), or work with small ensembles or individuals as needed.

> *Band Program 2:* small academically-oriented high school. Rigid scheduling allows for only one other music course in the curriculum. The course, called comprehensive musicianship, is offered five times a week. Students in band are allowed to elect the course any time during their four years in high school but not for more than two years. The great variances in individual differences that would obviously develop in such an arrangement are taken care of through the construction of sixteen levels of learning activity packets. These LAPS cover the fundamentals of music theory, basic conducting, the rudiments of orchestration, and composition. The class is organized so that students can work independently, in small groups, and in large groups. The latter arrangement is used for

occasional lectures, conducting assignments, and large group scoring projects. It is not uncommon in this class to find advanced students working on a one-to-one basis with less advanced students.

Band Program 3: large junior high school with an orchestra and chorus. Two full-time and one half-time music teacher. Students in this school who sign up for a performing ensemble are automatically enrolled in a music study laboratory. All three large ensembles are scheduled at the same time three periods a week (M W F). On alternate days (T and Th) all students meet together in the auditorium, where they are taught by a team of teachers who pool their talents to offer instruction in music theory, history, and literature. The availability of three teachers at one time allows for the breaking up of the large class into smaller groupings and dispersement to other classrooms. This school has two rehearsal halls and one classroom available at the same time.

Band Program 4: medium-sized, continuous progress school. One full-time music director and three part-time music specialists, brass, woodwind, percussion. Full band rehearsals are held four times per week (M T Th F). On Wednesday, the large group is divided into three small chamber ensemble classes. These classes are used mostly for special study unit work—creative projects, conducting, and chamber music. Music theory and history are offered through elective courses that use learning guides written by the music director. Scheduling of these courses is determined by the student in conjunction with the instructor (education by appointment). All instrumentalists in this program take private lessons for which they receive credit. When a student cannot afford to study privately, his lessons are paid for out of a special booster association fund that was established for that purpose.

Case studies such as these illustrate how scheduling patterns vary considerably from one school to another. No individual who is unfamiliar with a specific program can dictate by proxy the "ideal schedule." All one can hope to do is suggest ways to bring flexibility into the schedule. Case study number four is obviously an ideal situation; differentiated staffing provided excellent possibilities for flexible approaches to teaching and learning.

A fascinating futuristic look at the possibilities of teaching music through the utilization of flexible scheduling in conjunction with other educational innovations—programmed learning, team teaching, and technology—was reported some time ago by James A. Mason in an article titled "Music in the Continuous Progress School."[8] In Mason's hypothetical program, each student is allowed maximum opportunity to progress at his own rate of speed through a sequentially organized program of skills and concepts that interrelate performance with music theory, history, and the humanities. In this program, the student spends 40% of his time working alone; the remainder of his time is equally divided between small and large groups. In each learning situation, the student performs, analyzes, and listens to music; group discussions and reading assignments are also used. Two types of unique facilities are suggested for this program, prakti-booths and lecktro-booths. The prakti-booth is a small practice room equipped with a stereo headset, television screen, two-way communication to central control, and a stand that converts into a desk. The lecktro-booth is equipped with various electronic devices—stroboscope, dynalevel, tone analyzer, and tape recorder—that are used for developing specific performance skills. Both facilities are regulated by one person at a central control monitor, through which instructional software, recordings, audiotapes, films, and videotapes, can be transmitted to the individual booths upon request.

Teaching/Learning Strategies

Teaching/learning strategies are used to achieve specific instructional objectives. They are usually designed to involve students in activities that reflect musical behaviors found in society. For example, the student who writes a concert review or critique is actually performing the role of a music critic. Similarly, the student who scores his own composition for a chamber wind group is at once an arranger and composer; if he rehearses and conducts his own piece, he then becomes a conductor. Strategies can and should be designed to involve students in a variety of musical roles other than instrumental performance, the students' major preoccupation. Any valid musical behavior may be considered: music teacher, musicologist, theorist, listener, and so on.

Listening and Reading Assignments: Listening and reading assignments that are directly or indirectly related to a specific rehearsal/performance composition can be invaluable in helping students to know, understand, and perform that work. Whenever possible, listening assignments should include good recordings plus full and condensed scores. If the performance composition is a transcription, a recording of the original version should be used in addition to or in lieu of the transcribed version. Reading assignments may include analytical and historical notes prepared by the director, specific readings from one or more sources or, at least, record jacket notes and incidental notes included in the score. These materials should be made available so that students can complete the assignments outside of class at their own convenience but within a certain time frame—say one or two weeks before the concert performance of the work. Listening and reading assignments require a certain initiative on the part of students; if newly introduced to your program, it might be best to make these assignments optional. As students get used to the idea, they will inevitably recognize the value of completing the assignments. One band director who regularly placed listening and reading materials on reserve in the school library encouraged his students to complete the assignments without telling them if the assignments were required or optional. After taking a quick survey, he discovered that more than 60% of his band members were using the materials. Furthermore, the students commented that they found the materials helpful in their performance and enthusiastically supported the idea of continuing the assignments.

Projects in Creativity: One of the best ways to teach an understanding of the structural elements of music is through creative projects in which each band member is encouraged to experiment in the field of composition. You can start by asking each student to write a melody for his own instrument in a style similar to the melodic style found in a specific rehearsal/performance composition currently undergoing analysis. Time permitting, each student should be given the opportunity of playing his own melody in class. Selected melodies should be analyzed by the entire ensemble. Follow-up activities could include the composing of harmonic accompaniments to the best of these melodies and the scoring of the compositions for specific instruments. Young people naturally enjoy creative projects in composition; when given the proper stimulus and guidance by the director, some students can achieve amazing results.

Arranging and scoring projects are directly related to the teaching of the structural element of orchestration, or, more appropriately, bandstration. Again, these projects can be carried out concurrently with the study and analysis of a rehearsal/performance composition. If a more thorough study is desired, arranging and scoring can be taught as a special study unit (see Chapter Five). Another alternative is to offer an informal, noncredit course in arranging and scoring.[9] This class could be scheduled once or twice each week either before, during, or after school for as long as is necessary. A mini-course covering arranging for the clarinet choir, for example, might last one month; a more extensive course covering scoring for brass and percussion instruments might last **two** or more months.

Success in using arranging and scoring projects is dependent upon the band director, who must provide students with detailed guidance for each step of the way. This guidance may take the form of information sheets covering instrument ranges and transpositions, and worksheets with practical exercises for developing skill in transposition and scoring. To save time, these materials could be designed into a learning guide similar to the one given on page 85.

To achieve maximum student growth through the use of creative projects in composition, arranging, and scoring, every effort should be made to (1) play all student projects, however simple; (2) allow students to rehearse and conduct their own works whenever possible; (3) tape-record all projects—the tape should be made available so that each student can objectively evaluate what he has done; and (4) perform in public exceptional student projects worthy of a wider audience.[10] When advertised to students, these operational guidelines provide bandsmen with the necessary motivation to attempt and complete a creative project. One wind player who had composed several chamber pieces prior to the time he entered tenth grade in high school was encouraged and guided by his new band director to score one of his compositions for wind ensemble. He was promised that, when completed, the work would be rehearsed and taped. The project took six months to complete with the director providing only limited assistance. Because the composition turned out so well, the entire ensemble voted to perform the work at the next scheduled concert. This example illustrates what can happen when students are given encouragement to express their considerable creative potential.

Band Projects:[11] Band projects are used to enrich the musical diet of band members and to provide for individual differences. Assigned at regularly spaced intervals, these projects are usually completed outside of class. For each grading period, every band member is required to complete at least one band project of his own choosing from an approved list of projects provided by the director. The list, along with detailed instructions for completing each project, should be included in the source/reference notebook. The following list outlines several projects in wide use today.

A. *Research Reports.* Possible topics to include:
   1. a biography of a composer or professional musician
   2. the history of the student's musical instrument
   3. a historical style period or specific movement within a style period: neoclassicism, nationalism, impressionism

   In lieu of a written report, or in addition to it, students should be allowed to construct large wall charts based on the fruits of their research. In one junior high school visited by this writer, almost every wall surface in the rehearsal hall was covered with student-made charts. Topics ranged from illustrations of early flutes and hunting horns to time frame diagrams of historical periods and maps pinpointing the birthplaces of important European composers. Also displayed were many technical charts showing alternate fingerings, slide positions, snare drum rudiments, and so on.

   One or two highly qualified students should be regularly assigned to assist the director with the task of researching, writing, and editing program notes. These students should be exempted from having to complete band projects because they are, in effect, doing the same thing.

   As an alternative to the research report, students should be provided with an approved list of available books if they prefer to read a book and write a book report. Books like Aaron Copland's *What to Listen for in Music* and *Modern Music* by John T. Howard and James Lyons are suitable reading for young people and typical of what the list should include. In place of a book report, students could also be given the option of reading three or more articles of interest in music journals, magazines, or newspapers.

Written resumes covering the highlights of these readings should be turned in to the director and brief oral reports of selected articles should be presented to the entire band.

B. *Concert Critiques, Record Reviews, or Analytical Reports.*
Here the student is asked to attend a live concert and write a critique or listen to two different recordings of a given work and write a comparative review of the performances. As an alternative to this project, some students should be allowed to complete simple analytical reports. This alternate assignment may take the form of a flow chart analysis of a specific composition, a comparative analysis of one or more structural elements in two different compositions, or a harmonic analysis of a short movement of an extended work. Analysis generally requires rather complex analytical skills; consequently, this alternative project may be too difficult for the average school bandsman. If performance compositions are regularly analyzed in the rehearsal laboratory, however, at least a few bright students should be able to analyze a composition using models provided by the director.

C. *Solo or Chamber Music Performances.* A solo or chamber music performance may be considered a special project when prepared by the student of his own initiative outside of class. The subject is covered later as a separate teaching/learning strategy.

The important thing to remember when using band projects is that students need to be given several options from which to choose. The triple-option plan, requiring each band member to complete one of three alternative projects, a concert review, research report, or chamber music performance, works very well in both junior and senior high schools. Since it is virtually impossible to include all worthy projects in any plan, or even to be aware of the diverse interests and talents of a large group of students, it seems advisable to allow some students the option of devising their own projects with the approval of the director. These may include: (1) the construction of a primitive musical instrument, such as a bamboo flute, or a piece of needed musical equipment—percussion tray, telescopic music stand, and so on; (2) the preparation and presentation of a short teaching unit; or, (3) the design and construction of a bulletin board display. Suggestion (1) above could be expanded to allow students who possess special mechanical abilities and enjoy working with their hands the possibility of repairing school-owned instruments and equipment as a special project. With suggestion (2), each first chair player prepares and presents a ten-minute class demonstration, a sort of mini-clinic covering the unique characteristics of his instrument (technical problems, tone color possibilities, acoustical properties), and performs one or two short excerpts of representative solo literature. This project was used annually by one high school band director to sensitize his students to the unique characteristics of each instrument in the band. Teaching projects need not be confined to instrument unit presentations. Advanced students who possess natural teaching abilities should be identified early in the school year and assigned to tutor bandsmen who are experiencing difficulties. Less skillful performers can learn a great deal from older and more experienced players. Every effort should be made to utilize the considerable teaching talents of students through band projects.

Bulletin boards and wall surfaces of the rehearsal hall should be used to display student work and instructional material, to disseminate useful information, and, in general, to create a stimulating and aesthetically satisfying environment.[12] Students are ingenious at creating interesting and attractive bulletin board displays with a little guidance from the director. Here are two examples. (1) "The Honor Roll of Private Lessons" (see Figure 4). This display was designed by a junior high school student at the suggestion of his band director. The director wanted to recognize students who were already taking private lessons and to motivate those who were not. (2) "Tune in With Sine Nomine High School Band" (see Figure 5). Using cheerfully designed dust covers of new music, this high school student created an attractive and informative display of recently acquired band music. Similar displays could also be designed using record jackets and book covers of new music materials added to the school library. A "Current Events" bulletin board display

Figure 4

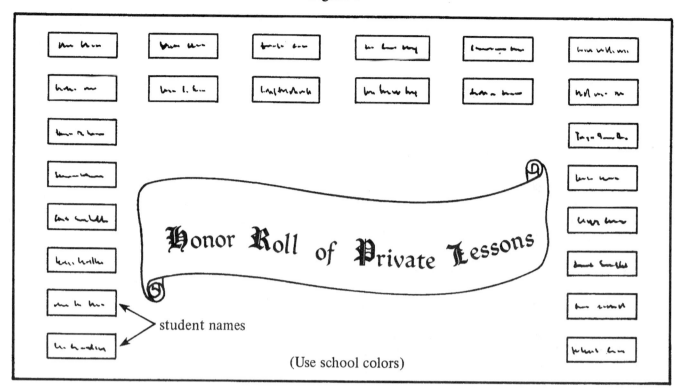

Honor Roll of Private Lessons

student names

(Use school colors)

Figure 5

TUNE IN WITH S.N. HIGH SCHOOL BAND

MCA

CP

MARCH

MUSIC

WINDS

HUSA

containing newspaper clippings of special musical events, programs and announcements of upcoming concerts, and similar materials should be established, with one or two students assigned the task of keeping the events current. This band project should be rotated periodically.

Conducting Assignments: Instrumentalists need to be able to recognize and respond to basic conducting patterns and styles in order to function effectively in any large performing group. Therefore, conducting assignments should be required of all band members to help them acquire basic knowledge and skill. Specific conducting objectives for all students are included in the special study unit learning guide given in Chapter Five. Ensemble rehearsals, sectionals, and other small instrumental music classes are ideal laboratory environments that should be used to provide as many students as possible with practical conducting experience. Individuals who demonstrate natural conducting ability should be designated as student conductors and given the opportunity to rehearse and conduct the full band. Student conductors should appear frequently on concert programs; and, whenever possible, they should help select the works they are to conduct. Conducting assignments give another dimension to music learning. Students generally find these activities highly stimulating and rewarding endeavors.

Group Discussions, Demonstrations, and Short Lectures: In the rehearsal laboratory group, discussions and demonstrations are periodically incorporated in the overall rehearsal routine. Discussion topics should relate to and grow out of specific rehearsal/performance compositions. Questions should be designed to elicit responses that help students grow in their knowledge and understanding of music structure, history, and style. An occasional, well-prepared lecture may be useful if used in conjunction with a class discussion; long-winded monologues are to be avoided. Group discussions and short lectures can come alive if musical concepts are illustrated through the use of audiovisual aids and followed up with out of class assignments and mimeographed study materials.

Chamber Music Performance and Study Activities: The organization and expansion of an active small ensembles program is of paramount importance in establishing a comprehensive musicianship curriculum. Chamber music activities should not be treated in a secondary or supplementary way. At the least, these activities should receive the same careful attention traditionally reserved for the large performing groups. The benefits to be derived from an active chamber ensembles program are many and worthy of detailed comment. Through chamber music activities:

—Students can be more evenly matched in ability and achievement. Each band member should be assigned to a chamber group with other students of similar ability. This will stimulate maximum musical growth within the ensemble and allow each performer to progress at his own rate of speed.

—Students can be exposed to an outstanding body of chamber music literature. Chamber music activities provide students with the opportunity to perform a wider variety of music representing different musical styles, historical periods, and idioms. Experienced band directors are well aware of the relatively limited body of quality literature available for the concert band. And, while the situation has improved considerably during the last two decades, the problem still remains because of the dearth of original full band literature representing earlier historical periods. With the establishment of a chamber ensembles program, however, a wealth of first-rate literature immediately becomes available for performance and study. Many early chamber wind works by outstanding composers, Gabrieli, Mozart, Haydn, Beethoven, Strauss, and others, are masterly artistic creations containing truly great musical ideas. Furthermore, these works are apt to be more abstract and less programmatic in content than full band compositions. Students who experience the pure joy of performing fine chamber music are not likely to be satisfied with playing second-rate band literature anymore.[13]

—Student musicianship can be developed much more rapidly.[14] Performing in a small group highlights for the student all of the important technical and musical problems that need to be dealt with in order to achieve a quality performance. Problems of intonation, phrasing, blend, balance, style, ensemble, tone quality, and technique are exposed and intensified to a degree unmatched in a large group setting. Quickly, students become keenly aware of their own musical and technical deficiencies. With one player on a part, each performer is challenged to carry his own part with technical accuracy and control and to improve his sight reading and listening skills. In meeting this challenge, the student begins to develop independence, self-confidence, and poise. In addition, the student is likely to become intrinsically motivated by the sheer pleasure of performing interesting, or at least novel, literature in a small group setting. The instrumentalist who has been trained to perform satisfactorily in a chamber ensemble is an invaluable asset to any band and will contribute greatly to improving the overall performance level and musicality of a large group.

—Students are more likely to develop the lasting habit of performing in small groups that will carry over to community and home life and continue after gradua- tion. If a student instrumentalist regularly performs in a chamber music ensemble while in school, he will probably continue to do so after graduation; thus, one major goal of the curriculum as stated in Chapter One will have been achieved— "playing music for enjoyment in small groups."

In addition to these major benefits, there are at least two important minor benefits to be derived from an active chamber ensembles program. First, by including chamber music groups with the full band on the same program, the director can bring variety into his concerts, and, at the same time, relieve some of the pressure of having to prepare an entire program of full band literature. Second, with the availability of numerous chamber ensembles, the director can readily respond to requests for performing groups to play at school and community functions. In terms of public relations and fund raising alone, an active small ensembles program is "worth its weight in gold"; many band directors raise funds by providing live chamber music for parties, businesses, and social functions.

In establishing or expanding a small ensembles program within the total band curriculum, the director may need answers to a number of perplexing questions. Which groups should be organized first? How will these groups be organized and trained? How can these groups be scheduled? Since most secondary school band programs are unique operations, answers to these questions are varied and complex. In determining which chamber ensembles to organize first, each director has to carefully analyze the talent within his pro- gram; the personnel available will dictate the ensemble groupings. There are many possibilities for small, medium, and large chamber ensembles. Small ensembles may consist of like instruments (flutes, clarinets, saxophones, trumpets, horns, and trombones); heterogeneous combinations within a family group, such as brass trios (trumpet, horn, and trombone), quartets (two trumpets, two trombones), and quintets (two trumpets, horn, trombone, and tuba); or, mixed instrument combinations crossing family groups, such as the standard woodwind quintets and sextets, for which there is an excellent body of literature available. Small ensembles such as these should be organized first since they provide the fastest road to developing student musicianship. Medium-sized chamber ensembles consisting of from six to nine players may be organized depending on the literature selected. Large chamber ensembles with ten or more players may consist of intact instrument family groups, woodwind choir, percussion ensemble, clarinet choir, and brass ensemble, or heterogeneous combinations of brass, woodwind, and percussion instruments.

Major responsibility for organizing a chamber ensembles program rests squarely on the shoulders of the band director. To lighten that responsibility, students should be encouraged to form their own groups. Student-formed groups are usually very successful because instrumentalists with similar abilities tend to gravitate toward each other. Once a group is formed, one capable student within the group should be put in charge. The director should assist the students by helping them to find a place and time to rehearse and suitable literature; he should also serve as a coach when needed.

There are many ingenious ways to organize a flourishing small ensembles program without creating unmanageable scheduling problems. Here are a few suggestions with proven success:

—*The Instrumental Recital Class:* Organize an instrumental recital class and assure student participation in the class by requiring every member in the band to perform at least one approved solo or chamber music selection each year. Usually, the recital class is scheduled one day a week after school. Performance recitals may be held biweekly, monthly, or as often as is necessary; recitals should be open to the public.

—*The Sectional Rehearsal:*[15] Convert your sectional rehearsals into chamber music classes; this procedure should be followed regularly and not just during festival time. Consider, for example, the trombone sectional. How much more stimulating and exciting it would be for trombone players if their sectional rehearsals were used to rehearse original trombone choir music instead of the relatively uninteresting and monotonous trombone parts usually found in concert band literature.

—*The Honor Society:* Organize an honor society for outstanding student musicians and define as one of the club's primary objectives the performance and study of chamber music. The honor society is an excellent vehicle for recognizing outstanding musicianship and stimulating superior musical attainment. Membership in the society should be restricted to a select group and determined by strict criteria: demonstrated performance skills, musical knowledge and understanding, academic scholarship, and so on. Candidates for membership in the society should be nominated and elected annually by all members of the band. Of course, the honor society need not be confined to the study and performance of chamber music. In addition to sponsoring student recitals, the society could also sponsor demonstration recitals by professional or semiprofessional performing groups, discussions with artists, and guest speakers. A festival of contemporary music combining a series of recitals with lectures by guest musicians and artists is typical of the activities that could be sponsored by this club.

—*The Ars Antiqua Society:* Another chamber music club, similar to the honor society, is the Ars Antiqua Society. This group of student musicians would specialize in the performance of old music played on old instruments. You could start by purchasing a consort of recorders and encouraging your best woodwind players to perform on these instruments. In time, the society could expand to include crumhorns, sackbuts, cornettos, and other instruments. Contemporary reproductions of early instruments are readily available and not too expensive; in addition, there is a growing body of simple but beautiful music now published for these instruments. Talented student musicians are highly intrigued and motivated by this type of chamber music performance. On one occasion, this writer witnessed a superb concert by a group of high school musicians performing Renaissance and Baroque music on old instruments. While the idea may seem unusual to some directors, it is feasible.

The ideas suggested above are offered as an outline of successful approaches used by imaginative band directors in organizing a flourishing small ensembles program. Although the outline is by no means all-inclusive, each band director should be able to find at least one idea that would be applicable to his own program.

Utilization of Community Resources

Most communities in the United States contain a wealth of musical resources that can and should be tapped to broaden and enrich the musical experiences of band students. Yearly musical activities should be planned so that student instrumentalists are continuously brought into contact with outstanding musicians and musical personalities in the community. Here are a few ways you can do this: (1) take your group on a field trip, (2) invite guest musicians in to work with your group (conductors, soloists, composers), (3) establish a concert and lecture series, or (4) organize a workshop, clinic, or festival.

Field Trips: Field trips are useful teaching/learning strategies because they extend the classroom out into the community. A group visit to a concert or open rehearsal by a professional or semiprofessional performing ensemble is one obvious type of field trip. For several years, one upstate New York band director regularly provided school bus transportation to Rochester so his students could attend the Friday evening concerts by the Eastman Wind Ensemble. Although attendance was not compulsory, many students took advantage of the opportunity to hear fine literature performed by this outstanding musical organization. These concerts proved to be a continuous source of motivation and stimulation to his band members.

Field trips can be expensive and time-consuming; they should only be used with specific purposes in mind. A group visit to an electronic music laboratory at a local university, for example, would be appropriate if your band were rehearsing a composition for electronic tape and band. Other possible field trips might include a visit to a museum to examine old manuscripts and musical instruments, a tour of an instrument manufacturing plant to see how musical instruments are made, a trip to a recording studio to observe professional musicians at work, or a group visit to a cathedral organ loft to see and hear how a reconstructed baroque pipe organ operates. Field trips such as these become enjoyable educational experiences for students when they are directly or indirectly related to their class work. With a little imagination and planning, a wealth of community resources can be utilized to enrich the learning experiences of students.

Although the exchange concert is not usually considered to be a field trip, this event can be turned into a broad cultural learning experience like the field trip. Here is how to do it. One month prior to making the exchange, ask your civics of social studies teacher to draw up an itinerary of important cultural and historic sites in the community to be visited. Then plan your trip so that your group has time to relax and enjoy themselves on a sightseeing tour.

Guest Musicians: There are many fine professional, semiprofessional, and amateur solo performers in most communities who would be willing to perform in concert with a school band. Once a soloist has been engaged and rehearsals are under way, you can enhance the overall learning experience for your students by asking the guest performer to present a mini-clinic on some aspect of his performance—style of the music, performance technique, interpretation, or whatever.

In recent years, a small but increasing number of school band directors have established the practice of commissioning a new work for wind and percussion instruments each year. The idea is educationally sound and highly recommended. Although the commissioning of a new work may necessitate additional fund raising activties or the reordering of monetary priorities, one would be hard pressed to come up with a more worthwhile endeavor on which to expend funds. Very often a fine but little known composer is willing to accept a commission for a surprisingly small amount of money. Furthermore, many original works commissioned by high school bands have been published; so the composer who is offered a commission always has that rewarding prospect before him. Most college and university music departments have at least one or two composers on their staff who might be willing to accept a commission to write for a school band. Schools of music with graduate departments may also have several capable students majoring in composition who could be considered as likely candidates for a commission. If, for whatever reason, it is impossible to commission a new work, the next best thing is to seek out and perform manuscript works by local composers. When feasible, the composer should be invited in to rehearse, conduct, and discuss his music with the performers. It is always an exciting educational experience for a student ensemble to rehearse and present a premiere performance of a new manuscript work, even more so if the composition was commissioned by the performing group and dedicated to them or to their director. Students usually develop a sense of pride in the realization that they have played an important and active role in the creation of a new art work.

Concert and Lecture Series: In addition to working with individual guest musicians, school bandsmen should be provided the opportunity of hearing skilled musical performances by outstanding performing groups from the community. To insure that your students receive this type of exposure, you can set up a yearly concert and lecture series and invite at least two or more performing ensembles to present concerts at your school.[16] Here again you should consider all community performing groups, especially military bands and college or university wind ensembles. The excitement and enthusiasm that can be generated through an excellent performance by a guest performing group cannot be duplicated easily by other types of school activities.

To balance out the yearly concert and lecture series, one or more guest speakers should be invited to discuss various music or music-related topics. For example, consider inviting a music critic, theorist, or musicologist; a music librarian, museum curator of old music and instruments, or music educator; a church musician; music industry field representative; an instrument repairman, piano technician, or recording engineer—the list is almost endless. Of course, presentations by individuals from the community need not be confined to formal lectures. Knowledgeable individuals who are visiting the school on official business should be invited in to the rehearsal hall to give informal talks to your groups. When the piano tuner is in the school, ask him to give an informal talk on some aspect of his work—equal tempered tuning, care and maintenance of pianos, career opportunities for piano technicians, and so on. If a university music supervisor is in the school to observe a student teacher, ask him to discuss career opportunities in music or degree programs offered at the college level. Formal lectures and informal talks can provide students with useful information that will help them to grow in their knowledge and understanding of music and music-related subjects.

Workshops, Clinics, and Festivals: The organization of a workshop, clinic, or festival is an excellent way to expose students to talented musicians in the community and, at the same time, to improve overall performance skills. A typical secondary school workshop could be organized to improve tone quality, intonation, or some other aspect of band performance. For a tone improvement workshop, several instrumental music specialists need to be engaged to cover various instrument groups within the band: high brass, low brass, single reed, double reed, and percussion. It would also be advantageous to engage one outside performing group, maybe a college chamber music group. This type of workshop is usually held on Saturday and runs all day long. Sessions should include the following: (1) master lessons by each of the specialists, (2) a demonstration and discussion period in which each band student performs a short prepared musical passage for the specialist, who in turn offers suggestions for improvement, (3) an open rehearsal, or a coaching and playing session, with the specialists sitting in while the school band rehearses under the band director's baton, and (4) an informal recital or concert by the guest musicians. The results of a tone improvement workshop are immediate and lasting and truly worth the time and effort involved in organizing the event.

Workshops and clinics are similar in that they both use specialists. The difference between the two is one of time, the clinic being a more compact and concise presentation. A few years ago this writer was engaged by a high school band director to run a sight reading clinic. The clinic was part of a winter weekend of musical activities held at a recreation camp. The clinic, which comprised two extended rehearsal periods, included a brief lecture and much practical work at sight reading. An outline of the lecture titled "Six Commandments for Developing Sight Reading Skill" was reproduced and distributed to the students for future reference.[17] This sight reading clinic was organized by the band director with two objectives in mind: (1) to encourage his students to develop a strong desire to improve their sight reading skill and (2) to provide them with specific guidelines for doing so. The overall objective of the three-day band camp, which included several other musical activities, was to expose the band members to knowledgeable and experienced musicians from within their community.

Another way to involve student musicians in cooperative musical activities with talented musicians from the community is to organize a high school wind ensemble festival. Concert and marching band festivals are common events in most city and county school systems. The high school wind ensemble festival, however, is a unique and novel idea. As the wind ensemble movement continues to grow in the United States, festivals of this type will gradually become more widespread.

The following is a first-hand description of a high school wind ensemble festival. The festival was sponsored by the instrumental music department of a large suburban high school located outside of Washington, D.C. The festival was held in the month of January and was the first of its kind in an area rich in musical resources. The band director of the sponsoring school is a highly respected musician and teacher with a reputation for developing excellent performing groups, particularly jazz and wind ensembles. He initiated the idea of a wind ensemble festival and organized the event. Letters of invitation were sent out to selected high schools in the area. To be accepted as a participant in the festival, each ensemble had to meet two criteria: (1) the size of the ensemble could not exceed fifty-five players, and (2) only original wind band literature could be performed (three selections). A professional clarinetist was engaged to work with each of the five selected wind ensembles. Each group was allotted fifty minutes of rehearsal time. The clinician, who was also a fine conductor, was asked to work with each director and ensemble on anything that needed attention—style, intonation, rhythm, conducting technique, and so forth. All clinic sessions were open to students and directors. The clinic portion of the festival culminated in midafternoon with a demonstration/concert by a wind ensemble from a local university. This group traced the history of the wind ensemble through the performance of selected wind literature from the Renaissance through the twentieth century. At the conclusion of the concert by the guest performing group, three high school wind ensembles were selected as semifinalists and invited to perform in the evening concert. After their performance that evening, while the judges were determining which ensemble would receive the first place prize of $150.00, the wind ensemble from the host school performed three selections. One of the selections was an original manuscript work for electronic tape and wind ensemble; the work was written by a local composer who was present in the audience. The festival proved to be a richly rewarding experience for all those who participated. The entire event was carried out in a relaxed, unhurried atmosphere, with each group given plenty of time to get involved.

The ideas suggested here on the utilization of community resources are offered as a potpourri of successful approaches used by practicing band directors whose programs are as diverse as the ideas themselves. The common thread running through all of these ideas is the conscious or subconscious desire of each band director to expose his students to musical talent in the community and thereby enrich their musical diet.

Miscellaneous Strategies

One important, albeit secondary, responsibility of the band director is to musically educate those who are not directly involved in the music program—parents, teachers, administrators, and the general student body of the school. The band director does not work in isolation; he must constantly strive to develop and improve the support of the school and community and, at the same time, try to raise the appreciation levels of his audiences.[18] The following ideas are offered as miscellaneous strategies that have been used successfully in the past to accomplish these ends.

The Band Parents Night: Here is a first-hand description of how to involve your band parents in a musically satisfying and educationally rewarding experience:

> In March of each year, a Band Parents Night is held for all band families. . . . The
> evening begins with a dinner for all and is followed by a talk by a guest speaker
> and the election of the new Band Parents Club Officers for the coming year. During
> the evening, parents visit different exhibits and demonstrations, attend a recital,
> see movies on band camp and the marching band, participate in a Band Parents
> Band, attend a rehearsal of the concert band. The evening ends with the parents
> who play instruments joining the students in a session of reading through some
> music together.[19]

The Music Appreciation Assembly: As an integral part of the comprehensive musicianship curriculum, the band director should plan a yearly sequence of music appreciation concerts for the total student body. These presentations should be organized around a central musical idea or topic and should include oral or written program notes.[20]

Weekend Festival of the Arts: Arts festivals are cooperative educational endeavors involving several departments within a school: music (instrumental and vocal), physical education (dance), English (literature, drama, poetry), and art. Arts festivals may last two or three days or one or more weeks depending on the scope of the theme.

Cluster Concerts: In recent years, several school systems in the United States have established cluster concerts. A cluster includes several elementary and junior high schools that feed one high school. A major goal for the music teachers of a cluster is to organize a concert in the spring involving music classes and performing groups from all school levels. The idea has great merit. What better way is there to develop bonds of communication between music teachers and to coordinate and integrate the music curriculum vertically?

In concluding this chapter on educational strategies, it should be emphasized that the key factors in a comprehensive musicianship program are flexibility and diversity. If a curriculum is to be effective in the rehearsal hall, it must contain different ways of activating students through a stimulating musical environment. As Jerome Bruner points out, "A curriculum. . .must contain many tracks leading to the same general goal."[21]

Footnotes (Chapter Two)

[1]For a recommended list of facilities, equipment, and materials, see *Guidelines in Music Education: Supportive Requirements* (Washington, D.C.: Music Educators National Conference, 1972).

[2]One imaginative band director made available part of his personal library of books and records for student use by setting up a circulation system through his office with one student assistant in charge. This same director also set up a magazine rack in the rehearsal hall on which he placed all of his back issues of *The Instrumentalist* for his students to read at their leisure.

[3]For a recommended bibliography and discography of library reference materials, see Karl Ernst and Charles Gary, *Music in General Education* (Washington, D.C.: Music Educators National Conference, 1965). This book is a valuable source of ideas for teaching comprehensive musicianship through eleven content areas that correlate well with the Blueprint of Objectives given in Chapter One.

[4]Sources for securing band recordings are listed in Appendix B. The Schwann Catalogue and other standard record catalogues should be consulted for all other recordings. For an extensive catalogue of miniature scores, write to Edwin F. Kalmus, P. O. Box 1107, Opalocka, Florida 33054.

[5]Band students generally spend from three to five hours per week in regularly scheduled rehearsals for from six to seven years in junior and senior high school, not counting extra rehearsals, sectionals, and concerts. Mercer reports that 55% of the high school band directors surveyed in his study held extra rehearsals outside of school time during concert season (Mercer, *op. cit.*, p. 21).

[6]Charles S. Peters and Paul Yoder, *Master Theory Series* (Kjos Music Company) contains six self-instructional workbooks—Beginning, Intermediate, and Advanced Theory; Elementary and Intermediate Harmony; and Advanced Harmony and Arranging. The workbooks can be used to "enrich band experiences" and "enhance ensemble performance."

[7]See Charles H. Benner, *Teaching Performing Groups: From Research to the Music Classroom No. 2* (Washington, D.C.: Music Educators National Conference, 1972), pp. 8-10. For an excellent overview of innovative scheduling practices throughout the United States, see Robert H. Klotman, *Scheduling Music Classes* (Washington, D.C.: MENC, 1968).

[8]*The Instrumentalist* (November 1965), Volume XX, No. 4, pp. 59-61.

[9]The informal, noncredit course can also be used to teach conducting, composition, secondary instruments (including piano), or almost any legitimate musical subject, provided there is sufficient student interest. The only restrictions that need be placed on students who volunteer or are invited to take the class are that they attend all classes and complete all assignments.

[10]A recital of original works conducted and performed by students before a PTA or parent booster association meeting can be tremendously stimulating for performers and listeners alike, not to mention the benefits that can be derived in terms of public support.

[11]Composition, arranging, and conducting assignments could also be used as band projects but have not been included here because they are covered elsewhere as separate strategies.

[12]There are many useful instructional charts and posters commercially available today. The Instrumentalist Company (1418 Lake Street, Evanston, Illinois 60204) and J. Weston Walch, Publisher (Box 658, Portland, Maine 04104) publish several excellent charts.

[13]Whenever possible, chamber ensemble members should be allowed to select their own performance literature; this should help students develop their analytical and judicial faculties. The director's responsibility is to make available a large library of chamber music for performance and study. See Appendix C for a selected list of chamber music compositions.

[14]Statistical evidence from Mercer's study indicates that preparing soloists and ensembles for contests is significantly related to the number of contests won by the concert band. Mercer concludes: "It seems reasonable to assume that a director who prepares many soloists and ensembles for contests will have a more polished performer for his large group." Mercer, *op. cit.*, p. 77.

[15]This suggestion is workable only if a rotating sectional rehearsal schedule is in use.

[16]The concert and lecture series could be organized and sponsored by an honor music society or some other music club.

[17]The Commandments are given on page 88.

[18]To increase the size of your audiences, ask each band member to invite one other family to concerts in addition to his own.

[19]Quoted from a pamphlet titled "The Ithaca High School Total Band Program" that was distributed at the Music Educators National Conference Convention, Chicago, Illinois, 1970.

[20]For detailed suggestions and guidelines on how to execute this strategy, see Labuta, *op. cit.*, pp. 220-225; and, *Music in General Education*, *op. cit.*, pp. 193-195.

[21]Jerome S. Bruner, *Toward a Theory of Instruction* (Cambridge, Massachusetts: Harvard University Press, 1966), p. 71.

CHAPTER THREE

THE SCORE: NUCLEUS FOR TEACHING AND LEARNING

In the Blueprint of Objectives given in Chapter One, the performance score provides the nucleus from which all objectives flow. Hence, the critical factor in building a comprehensive musicianship program is the selection of a qualitative body of literature for performance and study. In the performing ensemble, the repertoire represents the foundation of the curriculum.

Selecting the Repertoire

When selecting performance literature for your ensemble, carefully evaluate each selection to determine its teaching/learning potential as measured against the objectives of the blueprint. The repertoire must contain musical ideas that can be used to develop both concepts and skills. For discussion purposes here, each category of objectives will be covered separately as it relates to the selection of the repertoire. In actuality, however, the three categories are not segregated; any given composition may contain teaching/learning possibilities involving more than one category.

I. *Structural Elements:* The repertoire selected should illustrate a high degree of compositional skill or craftsmanship on the part of the composers. Many original contemporary wind band works that employ twentieth-century compositional techniques, modal harmonies, bichordal sonorities, serial procedures, and so on, are not truly great artworks that will withstand the test of time. While some of these works are well-constructed and suitable for performance and study by school music groups, one must be very careful in determining which works are valid and which are not. The typical director who is hard pressed for time is highly susceptible to catching a contagious disease that manifests its symptoms in what might be called the "bandwagon syndrome." Just because a work, or group of works, by a certain composer happens to be in vogue, that is, widely performed, it does not necessarily follow that the music is either good or great. The structural validity of a composition should be determined by the band director himself, using systematic procedures for selecting and evaluating new music.

II. *Historical Context:* The repertoire selected should illustrate man's mature artistic creations and represent diverse styles, forms, historical periods,and cultures. Selecting a broad spectrum of qualitative literature provides excellent teaching/learning possibilities through comparative analysis. Finding good original wind band music representing early historical periods, however, is a major problem.[1] Although the situation has improved over the last two decades through the research efforts of wind music scholars and musicologists, the problem still exists because the concert band is a performance medium of the twentieth century. In choosing music representing early historical periods, the band director inevitably has to come to grips with the long-standing debate over the pros and cons of using transcriptions and arrangements. It would be foolhardy to take a rigid position either way on the issue. In a practical sense, good transcriptions and arrangements may be the only way to expose students to the early master composers.[2] When transcriptions or arrangements of established masterworks for orchestra, keyboard, or other performing media are used, the original version should always be studied and listened to for comparative analysis. Indeed, band students should be encouraged to get involved in the debate over the use of transcriptions and to make value judgments concerning the validity of their use.

III. *Skills Development:* The repertoire selected should help to develop the musical skills of each bandsman. Skills development should always be thought of in terms of a threefold sense-orientation as outlined in the Blueprint of Objectives: aural (hearing), dexterous (tactile), and translative (visual). In selecting the repertoire, special consideration needs to be given to two specific aspects of skills development: technical proficiency (dexterous) and music sight reading (translative). In both areas, band directors have a tendency to select music that is too difficult for their students. Consequently, there is little or no time left for teaching and learning about other important aspects of music. This is an unfortunate state of affairs for many reasons, not the least of which centers on the fact that the most difficult music is not always the best choice. The problem could be eliminated by the director with a little forethought involving a careful evaluation of the proficiency levels of his students and a thorough analysis of the skills needed to perform a work.

In addition to the primary considerations listed above, there are several secondary considerations that may need to be taken into account when selecting the repertoire: audience appeal, student likes and dislikes, programming considerations, and so on. These considerations are usually of a functional or practical nature. And while they may loom large in some school and community environments, the band director must not lose sight of the importance of selecting a qualitative body of literature based on the primary objectives of the blueprint.

To aid the director in the difficult task of selecting the repertoire, a list of procedural guidelines is given below. The director who uses the guidelines will benefit in three distinct ways. First, he will be able to familiarize himself with a wide body of literature. Second, he will, in time, assemble a large collection of reference scores. Third, he will no longer have to purchase expensive new music (scores and parts) of unknown value and later discover that the investment was unwise. The system advocated here is less costly in the long run.

Procedural Guidelines for Selecting and Ordering New Music

1. Keep on file an open-ended master list of unfamiliar works. As the occasions arise throughout the year, add to this list those works that you come across; include as much information as possible when making the entry: title, composer, arranger, publisher, and difficulty. It is also a good idea to keep the programs of band concerts attended and to write notes in the margins on the works performed; drop these into master file for future reference.

2. Once a year, preferably in the late spring or early summer, compile a list of works from your master file that you want to study for possible use during the next school year. At this stage, order only a full and condensed score for each work.

3. After you have received the scores, study them at your convenience using the Evaluative Criteria Form given in Figure 6. Use good recordings for aural models whenever possible. A word of caution: many times a fine composition receives a poor aural impression on initial exposure. With conscientious study and analysis, the true worth and quality of a substantive work become obvious. Conversely, a composition that receives a good initial impression may wear thin with continual exposure and repeated listenings. The conclusion that may be drawn from this unusual situation is this: a valid way to determine the quality of a composition is to study, analyze, and listen to the work over a long period of time; if you continue to find creative and imaginative surprises in the music, the work probably contains substance.

4. After completing step three, you should be ready to order the literature for your ensemble. When ordering the music, be sure to purchase another set of scores for each selection. This will provide you with two sets of scores for each new addition to your performance library. The extra scores can be used for score study and listening assignments, analytical projects, conducting assignments, and adjudication purposes.

In summary, it should be re-emphasized that the selection of a qualitative performance repertoire is a critical factor in achieving the objectives of a comprehensive musicianship program. The task is unquestionably one of the most time-consuming, yet extremely important, aspects of the band director's work.

The Prelesson Plan Preparation

Before you can begin to prepare a lesson plan that focuses on the teaching of comprehensive musicianship through a selected composition, you need to have a thorough understanding of the structural elements of the composition and a general knowledge of the historical context within which the work was created. In recent years, several publishers have established the practice of including analytical and historical notes with their published band music. This practice is laudable and should be continued. Unfortunately, the quality and completeness of the information provided varies considerably from publisher to publisher. More often than not, the band director will have to complete his own analysis and historical research and write his own notes. Guidelines and procedures for completing both of these tasks are outlined below under the headings: "Analysis—Music Structure" and "Research—Historical Context."

Analysis—Music Structure: If you have followed the suggestions given under "Selecting the Repertoire" you should have a general understanding of the musical structure of the work to be analyzed and an aural impression of its sound.[4] Now it is time to make a thorough structural analysis of the composition.

Figure 6

Evaluative Criteria Form for Selecting New Music[3]

yes	no	unsure	
			I. ***Structural Elements (Craftsmanship):***
___	___	___	Does the work exhibit the craftsmanship of a skilled composer?
___	___	___	A. Are the melodic, harmonic, and rhythmic elements integrated, transformed, and developed in a skillful way?
___	___	___	B. Is the work expertly scored?
___	___	___	C. Is the form logically conceived?
___	___	___	D. Does the form shape the various elements of the work in a convincing way?

Comments: _____

II. ***Historical Context (Creative Expression):***

Does the work represent a mature artistic creation of man within the context of an identifiable stylistic period or culture?

A. Does the work reflect the ebb and flow of human emotions?
B. Does the work express deeply-felt human emotions?
C. Does the work contain abstract subtleties of expression?
D. Does the work contain extra musical ideas?

Comments: _____

III. ***Musical Skills (Aural, Dexterous, Translative):***

Does the work contain the potential for developing musical skills in a sequential way?

A. Aural skills? Identify and comment:

_____

B. Dexterous skills? Identify and comment:

_____

C. Translative skills? Identify and comment:

_____

IV. ***Additional Considerations:***

_____ Time?
_____ Beginning and ending keys or pitch centers?
_____ Grade of difficulty? Consider musical as well as technical factors. Use standard grading system or devise your own.
_____ Special instrumentation or resources needed?

(Use the reverse side for additional comments.)

When analyzing any specific structural element of a musical composition, always work from the whole to the parts and back to the whole again.

A_1 *Melody:*[5]

1. Locate and identify all important melodic ideas: main themes, subordinate themes, countermelodies, and so on.

2. Analyze the characteristics of each melodic idea in terms of its:
   - form: periods, phrases, motif
   - scale basis:
     conventional—major, minor, modal, whole tone, chromatic
     nonconventional—twelve-tone, serial, synthetic
   - dimensions:
     vertical—narrow or wide range
     horizontal—long, continuous line or short motival fragments
   - contour: direction (ascending, descending, combinations), contour patterns
   - progression: diatonic or chromatic, conjunct or disjunct
   - general qualities: lyric, dramatic, others
   - ornamentation: embellishments, coloration, figuration
   - additional considerations:
     prominence of certain rhythmic patterns
     prominence of certain notes or melodic intervals
     dynamic contour
     tone colors (instrumentation used)
     relationship of melody to texture
     relationship of melody to harmony, especially the use of nonharmonic
         tones in the melody: passing tones, neighboring tones, appoggiaturas,
         suspensions, anticipations, escape tones

3. Analyze the thematic transformation techniques employed:
   - inversion (mirror)
   - retrograde
   - retrograde inversion
   - augmentation or diminution (rhythmic variations)
   - tone color variations (varied instrumentation)
   - sequence
   - transposition
   - leitmotif
   - ostinato
   - repetition with variations of pitch, rhythm, timbre
   - combinations of the above

A_2 *Harmony:*[6]

1. Analyze the overall harmonic structure by identifying the beginning and ending key or pitch centers of movements and large sections.

2. Determine the harmonic or scale basis:
- major, minor, chromatic
- modal, whole tone, pentatonic
- polytonal, bitonal
- multitonal, microtonal
- pandiatonic
- synthetic
- atonal, serial, twelve-tone
- others

3. Analyze the internal harmonic movement:
- cadences (conventional—perfect, half, plagal, deceptive; or nonconventional)
- modulations (fifth, third, or second relationship types, others)
- progressions (intervals of root movement, sequence, parallelism—chord streams, elisions)

4. Analyze individual chord structures:
- tertian: built in thirds (triads—major, minor, diminished, augmented; sevenths, ninths, elevenths, thirteenths)
- nontertian: built in fourths (quartal), fifths (quintal), seconds (secundal)
- chord inversions
- chord alterations (omitted chord tones, added nonchord tones)
- bichords and polychords
- tone clusters and other dissonant chord structures

5. Additional considerations:
- prominent harmonic intervals
- harmonic rhythm
- harmonic tension (consonance versus dissonance)
  use of nonchord tones and added tones to create tension
  treatment of dissonance (preparation and resolution)
- relationship of harmony to melody

B. Rhythm:

1. Examine the overall tempo indications:
- relationships of tempos: similar and contrasting tempos
- use of tempo as a factor in establishing general moods:
  slow—tragic, majestic, heavy
  fast—gay, joyous, humorous, comical
- internal variations or changes of tempo: ritardandos, accelerandos
- interruptions of tempo: grand pause, railroad tracks, fermata

2. Examine the meters used:
- simple—duple (2/4, 4/4, 2/2), triple (3/4, 3/8, 3/2)
- compound (6/8, 9/8, 6/4, 12/8)
- asymmetrical or composite (7/4, 5/8, 7/8)
- polymeters (simultaneous use of diverse meters)
- changing meters, including meter expansion (2/4, 3/4, 4/4, 5/4) and contraction (7/8, 6/8, 5/8, 4/8)

- techniques used to obscure or destroy the pulse or meter: omission of bar lines, tying over bar lines, free rhythm

3. Identify special rhythmic devices utilized:
   - hemiolia (2:3 relationship)
   - syncopation

   augmentation

   - diminution
   - polyrhythms (simultaneous use of two or more complex rhythms)
   - thematic rhythms (nonmelodic)
   - ostinato rhythms
   - juxtaposition of diverse rhythm groups
   - note the use of rhythm to give drive, energy, and life to the music
   - note unusual uses of silence (rests)

C. *Bandstration:*

1. Analyze the score requirements to determine if any atypical instruments or musical resources are used.

2. Study the bandstration carefully by examining:
   - each family of instruments: woodwinds, brass, percussion
   - instrument choirs or sections: flutes, double reeds, clarinets, saxophones, conical brass (cornets, horns, baritones, tubas), cylindrical brass (trumpets, trombones), membrane percussion (timpani, snare drum, bass drum), cymbals, keyboard percussion, miscellaneous percussion
   - each individual instrument line

3. Note the use of:
   - special effects: mutes, flutter tongue, tremolo, glissando, quarter tones
   - extreme register scoring (high and low)
   - unusual unison or octave doublings
   - imaginative instrumental scoring combinations, for example, stopped horns and natural horns flutter tonguing in unison
   - contrasting tone colors
   - instrumental timbres for coloristic effects

D. *Dynamics:*

1. Study the overall dynamic scheme (movement and large section climaxes; subsection, period, and phrase climaxes).

2. Note the use of dynamic effects:
   - terrace dynamics
   - extreme dynamic ranges (ffff or pppp)
   - simultaneous use of contrasting dynamics
   - percussion instruments used for dynamic accent

- orchestrated crescendos or diminuendos
- subtle dynamic nuances
- quick changes of dynamics
- interweaving dynamics

E. *Texture*:

1. Identify and compare the musical textures utilized in the work:
    - monophonic (one line)
    - homophonic
        chordal ("familiar style"—note against note)
            number of parts
            spacing of parts
        melody with accompaniment
            sustained chord accompaniment
            repeated chord accompaniment
            arpeggio accompaniment (Alberti bass)
    - polyphonic
        number of parts
        relative importance of each part
        degree of melodic and rhythmic independence of each line
        spacing and crossing of parts
        imitation (note strictness and distance)
        devices: augmentation, diminution, stretto
        freistimmig (free voice writing)
    - hybrid textures (combinations of homophonic and polyphonic factors)
        solo (prominent melody) with polyphonic accompaniment
        quasi-contrapuntal style
        figuration
    - other considerations
        special textural effects (antiphonal, responsorial)
        use of counterpoint (parallel, oblique, and contrary motion)
        density (thickness or thinness of the musical fabric)

F. *Form*:

1. Analyze the "external" form to determine if the work belongs to a standard formal type:
    - sectional forms: binary, ternary, rondo, arch form (ABCDCBA)
    - variational forms: theme and variations, passacaglia, chaconne
    - developmental forms: sonata allegro
    - imitative forms: fugue, canzona, ricercare
    - stylized dance forms: bourrée, minuet, gigue, gavotte
    - free forms:
        sectional—toccata, prelude, fantasia, rhapsody
        based on extra musical ideas—poem, story, play, mythology
    - compound or multimovement forms:
        instrumental—concerto, suite, symphony, sonata, divertimento
        vocal and instrumental—cantata, oratorio, mass
    - hybrid forms (combinations of the above)

2. Analyze the "internal" form, sections, periods, phrases, in relationship to the melodic and harmonic materials.

3. Other considerations:
    - balance (symmetry)
    - unity (coherence, continuity)
    - variety (contrast)
    - number and relationship of movements
    - time factors (total length of movements or large sections)

4. Construct a flow chart of the internal form of the music. A flow chart is a clear and concise schematic diagram illustrating the interrelationships of the various structural elements of a composition. Constructing a flow chart for each composition analyzed is highly recommended. The chart can be used as an aid in memorizing the score and as a teaching/learning tool. The flow chart may be simple or detailed, depending on the complexity of the musical composition and the levels of understanding of those who will use it. The basic format for constructing a flow chart is given in Figure 7. A sample flow chart is given in Figure 8.

Research—Historical Context: The next step in completing the prelesson plan preparation involves the researching of pertinent information necessary for developing a knowledge of the historical context of the work. This back-up research should focus on three related topics: the composition, the composer, and the historical style period.

A. Background information about the composition:

1. Find out about the circumstances surrounding the creation of the work, historical, cultural, social. Make special note of the relationship of the work to contemporary events.

2. Determine if the work is representative of a "school of composition" or a movement within a historical style period: nationalism, impressionism, primitivism, expressionism, neoclassicism, neoromanticism, jazz, twelve-tone, serial, aleatoric, electronic, experimental.[7]

3. Find out when, where, and for whom the work was composed. Include information about the first performance if possible.

4. Determine the nature of the work. Is it an independent piece of music (absolute) or is it based on an extramusical idea (programmatic)? If the work is based on an extramusical idea, be it a poem, story, painting, play, or whatever, look up the programmatic idea to gain a fuller understanding of the work.

5. Determine the purpose of the work. Is it an overture to a musical play, ballet music, religious music, others?

When researching background information, try to find written comments about the work by the composer. This type of information will usually throw light on the nature and creation of the work.

Figure 7

Flow Chart Outline

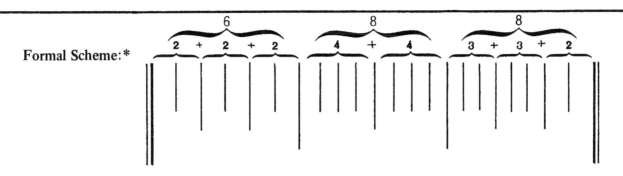

Formal Scheme:*

Melodic Design: Indicate main themes, subordinate themes, countermelodies, and so on (Th I$_a$, I$_b$, II, CM).

Rhythmic Elements: Include meters, tempo indications, and any important rhythmic ideas or devices.

Bandstration: Indicate instrumentation of thematic materials and important harmonic accompaniment materials. Use abbreviations: solo trp, tutti br, cl & sax, and so on.

Harmonic Structure: Indicate tonal (key) or pitch centers and important cadences, modulations, progressions, chords, and so on.

Texture: If desired, indicate the basic textures of sections and subsections.

Dynamic Curve: Indicate important dynamics, especially climaxes. It may be helpful to include a graphic curve illustration of the overall dynamic scheme:

*a. Use double bars to mark off movements and large sections.

b. Use vertical bars of varying lengths to mark off subsections, periods, and phrases. The bar lengths should correspond to the relative lengths of the sections marked off.

c. Use horizontal brackets and numbers to indicate the number of measures enclosed in a section, period, or phrase.

d. For extended works or movements, it may be helpful to construct an abbreviated flow chart to reveal more clearly the external form of the music.

Figure 8

"Song of the Blacksmith" from *Second Suite* by G. Holst

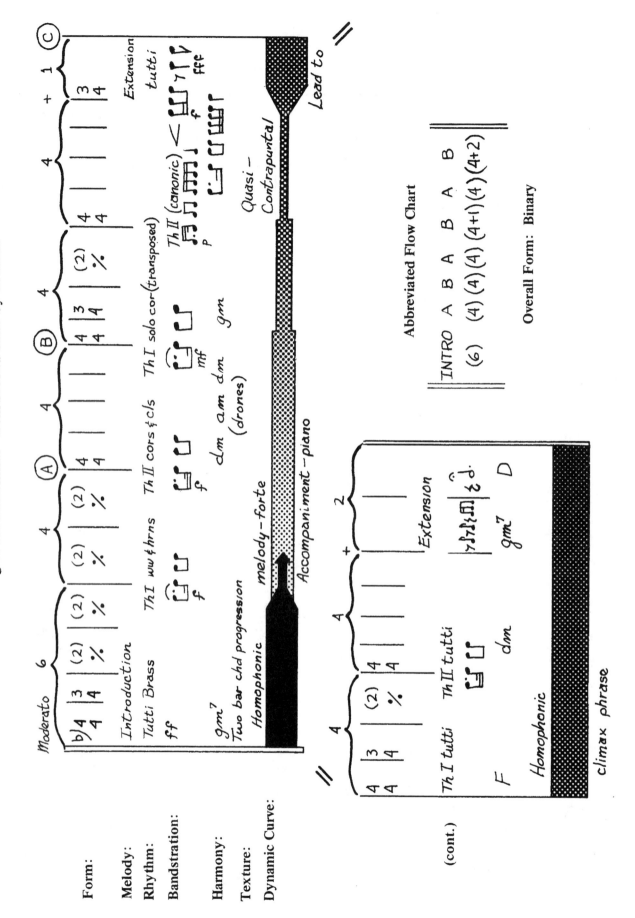

Abbreviated Flow Chart

INTRO A B A B A B
(6) (4) (4) (4) (4+1) (4) (4+2)

Overall Form: Binary

B. Biographical information about the composer:

1. Composer's place and date of birth and death.

2. General information about the composer's life and work.

3. Composer's contribution to the history of music and the evolution of music composition.

C. Stylistic and performance practices of the historical period that the composition represents.

1. The role of the performer and the performance medium.

2. Style characteristics of the period related to the performance and interpretation of melodies (ornamentation, articulations, phrasing, timbres), rhythms and tempos, and dynamics.

3. Other period characteristics relating to forms, textures, harmony, and instrumentation.

When completing the back-up research, keep an accurate log of sources consulted; this information may be needed later when writing the lesson plan materials. Sources may include biographies, music history books, dictionaries and encyclopedias of music and musicians, books on style and performance practices, and music journals. Some journals, for example the *Journal of Band Research,* periodically publish excellent analytical articles on standard wind band compositions.

The final step in completing the prelesson plan preparation involves the compilation of a glossary of the musical terms that appear in the score or are in some way related to the musical structure and historical context of the work. The list should contain all terms that may be new or vaguely familiar to your students. Since the glossary will be used for instructional purposes, clear and concise definitions should be included. Don't forget to include musical terms that appear as titles of works and movements: suite, symphony, divertimento, concerto, gigue, intermezzo, chaconne. These terms are especially important in helping students develop a conceptual understanding of the music they are performing.

After completing the prelesson plan preparation, you should be ready to begin building the lesson plan and writing the instructional objectives and activities. It is highly recommended at this point that you write a complete set of analytical and historical notes for the composition selected. The notes will be used extensively later on for instructional purposes in the rehearsal hall and for out of class reading and study assignments. The suggested outline for the notes is given below. The format is in reverse order of that given in the prelesson plan preparation because the historical notes serve as a general introduction to the work.

Title of the Work

Composer/Arranger

Publisher and Date

Recordings of the Work (Include record title, number, performing group and conductor.)

Historical Notes:
    The Composition
    The Composer
    The Historical Style Period

        When paraphrasing or quoting material verbatim, use footnotes
        (source, author, pages). Include sources for further reading and
        study if desired.

Analytical Notes:
Melody
Harmony
Rhythm
Bandstration
Dynamics
Texture
Form

> It may not be necessary to write analytical notes for every structural element listed. Include only those elements that illustrate important musical concepts that will be covered in the lesson plan.

The analytical and historical notes should be complete unto themselves and readable by the average school bandsman. Cryptic references to minute passages in the score should be avoided. Most score examples referred to in the text should be included in the notes.

At this point, it may be helpful to the reader to examine the material given in the next chapter. The chapter presents a model unit study composition complete with analytical and historical notes, lesson plan, and student study guide.

Building the Lesson Plan

A three-part format is suggested for use in building the lesson plan: (1) concepts, subconcepts, and objectives; (2) activities for teaching comprehensive musicianship; and (3) evaluation.[8] This format is highly recommended in that there is continuity and integration of all phases of the teaching/learning process for each unit study composition. Although the specifics of each lesson plan vary from composition to composition, the overall format remains the same.

Selecting the Concepts and Subconcepts: The structural elements of music outlined in the Blueprint of Objectives—melody, harmony, rhythm, bandstration, dynamics, texture, and form—provide the basic core of seven musical concepts upon which to build the lesson plan for each selected composition. To this basic core of concepts, an "additional concepts" category is added to encompass the historical context of the work and other important aspects of the work not covered elsewhere.

Subconcepts are specific, readily definable ideas that flow from and relate to the more general concepts. An understanding of the concept of harmony, for example, is developed through the study of specific aspects of harmony—the major triad, the perfect cadence, the tritone interval, the fifth relationship modulation, and so on. Other concepts are similarly developed through the use of subconcepts. A comprehensive list of subconcepts is suggested in the analytical guide given in the prelesson plan preparation. Determination of which concepts and subconcepts to include in the lesson plan should become apparent upon completion of the structural analysis of the work and the back-up research. Keep in mind that not all core concepts need be included in each unit study lesson plan. Select only those concepts and subconcepts that naturally flow from the selected work and dictate emphasis.

Writing the Instructional Objectives: The objectives included in the model lesson plan given in the next chapter are, for the most part, stated behaviorally and are operational at the instructional level. They are short-term objectives that identify what the student can be expected to do at the end of the instructional unit, approximately four to six weeks, or however long it takes to prepare the unit study composition for public performance. While it is not within the scope of the book to cover the writing of instructional objectives in any detail—the subject is thoroughly covered in other sources[9]—it is appropriate to include here a few comments concerning the construction and use of instructional objectives.

Instructional objectives are specific, unambiguous statements of desired learner performance. As such, they do not state what the teacher is to do, but rather, what the teacher expects the student to be able to do. To be properly stated in behavioral terms, an instructional objective should specify three things: (1) exactly what it is that the student who has mastered the objective will be able to *do*; (2) under what *conditions* the student will be able to do this; and (3) to what *extent* the student will be able to do this (the performance standard). In short, a well-written instructional objective should specify under what *conditions* and to what *extent* a certain kind of student *performance* can be expected to take place.

When writing instructional objectives, use only action verbs to indicate the behaviors to be observed:

arrange	*define*
compose	*notate* from dictation
transpose	*identify* aurally or visually
explain	*map* the form—flow chart
determine	*edit* the music
compare	*demonstrate* through performance—
transform	play, conduct, or sing
describe	

Certain phrases should be avoided because, by their very nature, they are so vague that they give no one a clear idea of what is meant:

create an awareness of	become aware of
develop a feeling for	become familiar with
develop an appreciation of	develop a knowledge of

Currently there is no way to objectively evaluate a student's "familiarity with," "appreciation of," or "feeling for" a particular subject. These words are unacceptable for use in instructional objectives; they do not clearly specify to anyone, teacher or student, what is expected.

There are many advantages to using instructional objectives for each unit study composition. The most important advantage is that their use in the curriculum will likely result in significantly higher student achievement levels. Dr. Williams states that "when teachers use instructional objectives as a basis of instruction, student achievement increases by a factor of approximately 50% over students that are not provided with instructional objectives."[10] Establishing instructional objectives for each unit study composition also helps in the organization of a mini-systems approach to music teaching and learning[11] by providing: (1) direction for developing continuity in each lesson plan from beginning to end (concepts, subconcepts, and objectives ——→ activities and assignments with options ——→ evaluation); (2) guidance in the selection and utilization of instructional software and hardware; and (3) a nonsubjective basis for assessing student progress.

Further, the use of instructional objectives:

—Provides for individual learning differences. A well-organized curriculum utilizing instructional objectives is student-centered rather than teacher-centered. The focus of the teaching/learning process is on the learner. Individual student learning styles, motivational states, interests, and potential are taken into account through the use of a variety of activities and assignments with options.

—Encourages the student to evaluate his own progress. In addition to providing the band director with an explicit and objective way of evaluating student perform-ance, instructional objectives also permit self-evaluation on the part of the student. To insure that each student recognizes and takes advantage of the opportunity afforded him for self-evaluation, the band director should reproduce the list of concepts and objectives for each unit study composition and distribute them at the beginning of the instructional period as part of the student study guide.

—Provides a basis for curriculum evaluation. Given a series of unit study composi-tions with stated instructional objectives, the band director can, with much greater accuracy, assess the content and value of his curriculum, diagnose areas of strength and weakness, and make revisions for improvement.

—Provides a basis for initiating teacher accountability. In this day and age, when many music teachers, ensemble directors included, have to justify their positions and sub-ject matter in the schools, or demonstrate their ability to raise the levels of achieve-ment of their students, instructional objectives can serve both situations well. Joseph Labuta accurately clarified the problem of accountability as it relates to the traditional performing ensemble director when he wrote: "Group performance alone is no longer accepted as a measure of musical accountability. Accountability means that music teachers are responsible for the learning of each pupil as an individual, as well as for the training of bands, orchestras and choruses."[12]

While there is much that can be said in favor of using instructional objectives in the curriculum, their use does not automatically guarantee success. Ronald B. Thomas summed up the situation in his final report on the Manhattanville Music Curriculum Program by stating:

No one can predict all of the outcomes or even the most important outcomes of any learning experience. At best the preparation of behavioral objectives can help in assuring that the curriculum has meaning and movement, that both the student and teacher will have direction and recognize progress. Some of this progress will be in terms of the stated objectives. Much of it will be in areas not covered by the objectives but related to the total experience. For the student, these unplanned discoveries may be his most significant learning.[13]

Designing the Activities for Teaching Comprehensive Musicianship: The activities selected for teaching comprehensive musicianship should be carefully designed to achieve the learning goals stated in the objec-tives; they should grow out of and be directly related to the predetermined list of concepts and objectives.

In designing the activities, the composition must be the point of departure in the rehearsal hall. Most in-class activities should start with the actual rehearsing of a specific passage of the unit study composition. Never lose sight of the fact that the work has to be prepared for public performance. To develop the skills necessary to perform the work, extract scales, chords, intervals, rhythms, dynamics, and articulations from the score and design them into warm-up drill activities. You can use dictated drills, selected exercises from standard technique books, or write your own materials. All drill materials should be included in the student study guide as a home practice assignment. The warm-up drill period at the beginning of the rehearsal is an excellent time to teach the structure of the unit study composition and to sharpen aural skills; melodic, harmonic, and rhythmic dictation should be periodically included in the planned activities.

To provide for individual learning styles, the activities should include a variety of instructional resources and assignments with options. The resources utilized in the model lesson plan, for example, include the following materials and audiovisual equipment: analytical and historical notes, scores, records, and tapes; tape recorder, record player, opaque projector, piano, and chalkboard. These resources are designed into the activities so that their use does not interrupt the flow of the rehearsal. The optional assignments included in the student study guide were designed so that they could be accepted as band projects. In most cases, these assignments are extensions of creative activities. Every unit study composition should have at least one simple creative assignment that is open-ended. Gifted students should be encouraged to develop these creative projects into more sophisticated forms.

The glossary of musical terms compiled during the prelesson plan preparation should be included in the student study guide and distributed during the first rehearsal of the unit study composition. A few of the terms should be left blank to encourage students to develop the habit of looking up unfamiliar musical terms on their own. To insure that each bandsman develops this basic research skill and is exposed to standard music reference sources, assign one or two students the task of looking up terms on a rotating basis. The definitions should be presented orally in class so that others may copy them in their notebooks.

Determining the Method of Evaluation: Implied or stated in a well-written instructional objective is the method for evaluating mastery. If the activities for teaching comprehensive musicianship are designed to achieve the learning goals stated in the objectives, there should be no trouble in assessing student growth. Most activities will be evaluated daily during the instructional period. In and out of class assignments, creative projects, written and oral quizzes, and dictation work produce concrete evidence for the evaluation of student achievement in terms of stated objectives. In addition, it is recommended that a final unit examination be given at the end of the instructional period for each unit study composition. The final exam, not to exceed one rehearsal period in length, should include some form of listening related to the unit work. Overall assessment of student learning should weigh in favor of the daily evaluations, with the final unit evaluation receiving less emphasis.

In conclusion, it should be noted that the lesson plan outline suggested here is only a model, so it can be freely adapted, simplified, extended, or modified. One important activity that could be added, for example, is comparative analysis. After completing lesson plans for two or more unit study compositions, comparative analysis should be initiated. Even with only one lesson plan completed, some comparative analysis can be initiated, using concurrent rehearsal/performance compositions.

Since it would be impractical to write a detailed lesson plan for every composition in preparation at any given time, it is recommended that only one work be selected from each projected concert program for intensive study via the unit study lesson plan. In this way, approximately three or four lesson plans can be completed each year without a drastic disruption of established rehearsal routines. Over a period of a few years a solid core of curriculum materials could be established for teaching comprehensive musicianship through band performance.

Footnotes (Chapter Three)

[1] For a selected list of early wind band music, see Appendix C.

[2] One way to circumvent the overuse of transcriptions is to expand and develop your chamber music program. There are many fine musical compositions available for chamber wind groups of various sizes and instrumentation from the Renaissance, baroque, classical, and romantic periods. See Part II of Appendix C.

[3] With slight modification, this Evaluative Criteria Form could also be used by students when making value judgments about the music they are playing.

[4] Be careful not to rely heavily on one recorded performance of a work for your aural model. If the performance is not true to the score, an inaccurate impression may become fixed in your mind. If possible, try to listen to two or more different recordings of the same work and compare the interpretations in relationship to the score indications. It is not uncommon to find discrepancies of tempos, style, and interpretations in recorded performances of standard wind band music by recognized conductors and performing groups.

[5] This outline correlates with the clarification of the Blueprint of Objectives given on page 3.

[6] For compositions written in a traditional harmonic style, use conventional chord symbols (Roman numerals I_4^6 V^7 I). For nontraditional harmonic compositions, identify individual chords or chord members by their letter names—tertian chords ($D^{\flat 9}$, G^{add6th}, e mi^{13}), bichordal sonorities ($[_C^{e\flat}]$), quartal harmonies (Qt. C F $B^\flat$ $E^\flat$), clusters (Cl. C $C^\flat$ D $D^\flat$ E). For assistance in analyzing contemporary compositions, see Leon Dallin, *Techniques of Twentieth Century Composition* (Dubuque, Iowa: William C. Brown Company, second edition, 1964); and Vincent Persichetti, *Twentieth Century Harmony* (New York: W. W. Norton and Company, Inc., 1961).

[7] An outline of the historical style periods of Western art music, including major composers, compositional forms and devices, and the like, should be provided in the source/reference notebook; see Appendix A, Part II B.

[8] This format is similar to the one developed by the Research and Development Group, College of Education, University of Hawaii, for the Hawaii Music Curriculum Project. See Appendix B under Comprehensive Musicianship Source Materials.

[9] Two highly recommended sources for further study are: *Instructional Objectives in Music: Resources for Planning Instruction and Evaluating Achievement,* compiled by J. David Boyle for the National Commission on Instruction of the Music Educators National Conference, 1974; and, *Establishing and Evaluating Instructional Objectives* by William W. Williams, Norton Publishers, 1970. The latter publication is a concise pamphlet on the subject written especially for busy teachers; for a copy, write to Norton Publishers, P. O. Box 1175, Riva, Maryland 21140.

[10] William W. Williams, *op. cit.,* p. 25.

[11] "Learn to Apply a Systems Approach in Music Education," *Music Educators Journal* (November 1971) Volume 59, Number 3, pp. 71-72.

[12] Joseph Labuta, "Accent on the Output," *Music Educators Journal* (September 1972) Volume 59, Number 1, pp. 43-49.

[13] Ronald B. Thomas, *MMCP Synthesis: A Structure for Music Education* (Elnora, New York: Media, Inc., 1971), p. 11.

CHAPTER FOUR

THE MODEL LESSON PLAN

This chapter presents a model lesson plan for studying a single composition. Included are historical and analytical notes, a unit study lesson plan with a final unit evaluation, and a student study guide.

Unit Study Composition: Spectrum by Herbert Bielawa

For prerecorded electronic tape and band.

Publisher: Shawnee Press Incorporated, 1967.

Recordings: Educational Record Reference Library 6
University of Redlands Symphonic Band
James Jorgensen, Conductor

Crest Records CBDNA 75-3
Brigham Young University Symphonic Wind Ensemble
K. Newell Dailey, Director

Crest Records CR-6001
Ithaca High School Band
Frank Battisti, Conductor

Historical and Analytical Notes

Historical Notes

The Composition: The composer speaks: *"Spectrum* was written in the spring of 1966 for the Memorial High School Band in Houston, Texas. The piece was written as part of my work under the Ford Foundation grant as composer-in-residence for the Spring Branch Independent School System [1964-66]. It is a work for mixed media, pre-recorded tape and live musicians, and is a serial piece in one movement of about five minutes in duration."[1] Since its first performance by the Memorial High School Symphonic Band under the directions of Gerald Clanton in the spring of 1966, *Spectrum* has been performed numerous times by high school and college bands throughout the country.

The Composer: Herbert Bielawa (b. 1930) is a native of Chicago. He holds three music degrees from the University of Illinois, Urbana. At the time *Spectrum* was published in 1967, Bielawa was working toward a Doctor of Musical Arts degree at the University of Southern California, while teaching full-time at San Francisco State College. Mr. Bielawa has written numerous works for different performance media. Among his recorded band works is the *Concert Fanfare,* a symphonic composition in a martial style (Educational Record Reference Library 28).

The Historical Style Period: Although *Spectrum* is a distinctly contemporary artwork, reflecting twentieth-century compositional devices and techniques, the work is not entirely divorced from tradition; cause and effect, unity and variety, exposition and development all operate in the composition. Bielawa explains: "Two aspects of the piece are. . .thrust beyond the traditional: the use of electronic sound and the use of cluster sonorities (in part a result of the serialization). To counterbalance the courtship of these two extremes, I have purposely kept the overall form of the piece rather straightforward, namely ABA."[2]

Performance and Interpretive Aspects of the Work: When performing *Spectrum,* careful attention must be given to the complex motor rhythms dominant throughout the work; these must be performed accurately, that is, turned on and off with precision. Further, cluster sonorities and melodic fragments must be properly balanced to achieve the intended polyphonic web of kaleidoscopic color sonorities— "polyphony of musical gestures." Careful attention must also be given to the performance of articulations, especially simultaneous use of contrasting articulations. Staccatos are to be played secco, that is, very short and dry; tenuto staccatos (⁻) are to be played detached, about a full eighth note in length. Sforzandos should be played with an explosive attack and marcatos should be strongly marked with a clean ictus at the beginning of each note. Other important interpretive aspects of the work are covered in the analytical notes that follow.

Analytical Notes

Melodic and Harmonic Tonal Organization: Spectrum is tonally organized by the following three-part series:

Example 1

The first two parts of the series contain five notes each, the second part being the exact inversion of the first at the interval of a fifth. The third part of the series comprises only two notes a semitone apart. All twelve chromatic tones are included in the series. According to the composer, the serial organization "reaches into the pre-recorded electronic pitches as well as the performed parts."[3]

Four important musical ideas, called "gestures," are used in *Spectrum.* The first is a broad quarter-note triplet figure heard at the beginning in the horns:

Example 2   Gesture I

The second gesture, "sustained texturized tones," is also heard at the beginning:

Example 3   Gesture II

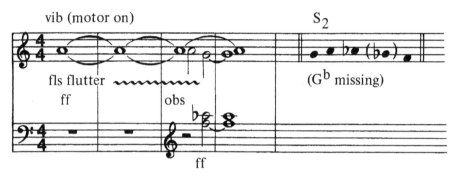

Gesture three is a "dialogue between cornets and clarinets":

Example 4   Gesture III

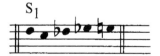

48

The fourth gesture, a series of "broad ejaculatory tone cluster sonorities," uses extreme register scoring:

Example 5   Gesture IV

All melodic fragments found in *Spectrum,* such as those given in Examples 2 and 4 (Gestures I and III), are derived from the three-part series; these are transformed using standard serial techniques: inversion, retrograde, retrograde inversion, and transposition. Example 6 illustrates the use of the retrograde form of part two of the series:

Example 6

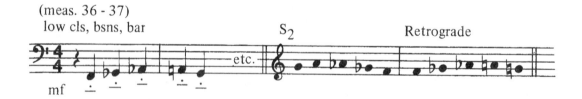

Example 7 illustrates the use of the inverted form of part one of the series at the interval of a major seventh; the inverted form may also be viewed as a transposed version of part two of the series (down a major third):

Example 7

(meas. 23 - 24)

The disjunct tape ostinato passage (repeated five-note group) illustrated in Example 8 is also based on part one of the series:

Example 8

(meas. 161 - 191)

The harmonic sonorities found in *Spectrum* are nontertian (there are no triads or seventh chords) and very dissonant. Chord structures are derived from the three-part series; see Examples 9a and 9b, and also Examples 3 and 5.

50

Example 9a

Example 9b

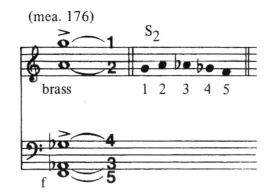

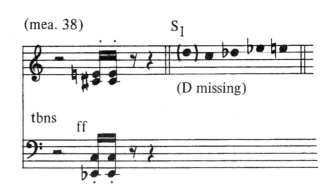

Tone cluster sonorities using almost all of the twelve notes of the series simultaneously are interspersed throughout the work:

Example 10   Tone Cluster

All notes of the series
included except D natural.

Dissonant intervals, major and minor sevenths and ninths, tritones, major seconds, are used to harmonize melodic fragments in parallel motion; Bielawa calls this "color doubling." See Examples 11 and 12, and also Example 2.

Example 11   Parallel Major Seconds

Example 12   Parallel Tritones and Major Sevenths

Rhythm: Tempo, Meter, and Rhythmic Devices

The meter and tempo indications found in *Spectrum* reflect the three-part formal scheme of the work:

Tempo I   (♩ = 152-160) Boldly with drive (band) $\frac{4}{4}$ time.

Brief electronic tape phrase into:

Tempo II   Slow feel $\frac{2}{2}$ | ♩♩♩ ♩♩♩ | (tape plus instruments).

Maestoso molto—brass lead back to:

Tempo I   Boldly with drive (band and tape) $\frac{4}{4}$ time.

Coda—tape fade out.

52

Changing meters are found in the tape part of the middle section, but these present no problems. An example of expanding meters may be found in measures 59 - 63 in the score (3/4 4/4 5/4). An unusual time signature is used in measure 114 ($^{1/2-1}_{2}$); this meter could have been written in 3/4 time. Because the horns play a quarter-note triplet on the latter part of the measure, the meter is performed with a fast down-beat quarter-note and a normal half-note upbeat:

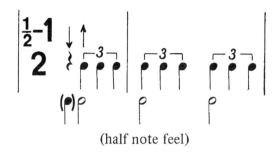

(half note feel)

Spectrum is very complex rhythmically. Cross-meter triplets and polyrhythms abound in the work:

Example 13   Cross-meter Triplets

(mea. 1)

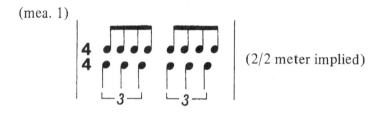

(2/2 meter implied)

Example 14   Polyrhythms

(mea. 10)

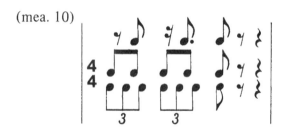

Bielawa also uses several rhythmic devices to obscure the normal pulse and meter; these include the use of tied notes (Example 15), disjunct ostinato-like rhythms (Example 16), and syncopations (Example 17):

Example 15

(meas. 183 - 187)

Example 16

(meas. 193 - 196)

Example 17

(mea. 179)   (mea. 181)

Bandstration: Concerning the band scoring, the composer says: "I have used the instruments in this piece as an artist would use paints, counting on the individual instruments to preserve their typical colors. This is, essentially, contrary to the philosophy of total blending of all instruments into a resultant organ-like tone."[4] The band instrumentation for *Spectrum* is standard. The only atypical musical resources required are a tape recorder, amplifier, and stereo speakers. Several special bandstration effects are used in *Spectrum;* these include:

1. flutter tonguing (flutes)

2. muted tone colors (stopped horns and muted trumpets and trombones)

3. percussion effects

     vibraphone (soft mallet rolls with the motor turned on)
     orchestral bells (double note rolls using brass mallets)
     bass drum (hard sticks)

snare drum (rim shot)
timpani (simultaneous glissandi on two different drums, see Example 18)

4. contrasting articulations (simultaneous use of flutter tonguing, tenuto staccato, and legato on the same melodic line by three different instrument groups; see measures 36-43 in the score)

5. extreme register scoring (tubas divisi, low F♯ and A, measures 5 and 6; horns unison a^4 in the high register, measures 40-43)

Example 18

Concerning the prerecorded tape sounds, Bielawa writes:

> The sources of all electronic sounds in the piece were a piano and white noise. They would therefore be classified as *musique concrete*. Transforming these sounds was done originally in Houston without the aid of any modular equipment (electronic filters, reverberation units, etc.). All transformations were made solely with the use of tape recorder manipulation and tape cutting. Recorder manipulation included speed changes, echo feedback, gain control, and reverse taping. Actual tape manipulation included cutting off attacks and decays from pre-recorded piano sounds and tape clipping. I also made use of several tape loops to create *ostinato* accompaniments throughout the piece.
>
> Incidentally, one other sound source. . .was created by scraping the microphone over the undampened strings of the piano. On the tape it makes a sound which I have referred to simply as "ching." . . .In preparing the tape part for *Spectrum,* my usual compositional procedures required the inclusion of a few new steps. A significant period of time was necessary simply to experiment with the sounds and tape manipulation. It was a period of discovery and the spirit of adventure ran high. It soon became evident that the exercise of restraint was imminent, since not all sound discoveries would or should be engaged in a given composition, lest one allow colors to supersede good taste and balance of dramatic forces in form.[5]

Bielawa comments further on the use of the tape *scorrevole* just before the return of section A (letters J to K in the score):

> The tape part is at this point a series of many tones at a dazzling speed and extremely high frequency (beyond the piccolo or piano range by some two octaves). This silvery glitter is punctuated by sforzando chords in the band. . . .[The effect is] to clear away section "B," [and] to get back to "A." . . . As it does, "A" rides in on the spent "froth" of the tape *scorrevole* which has now been quieted. . .[6]

Concerning the use of graphic notation for the electronic tape sounds, the composer asks:

> Why such unorthodox notation? Why notation at all? First, much of the electronic sound simply cannot be put in conventional notation. Second, notating the electronic sounds as I have makes it much easier to see at a glance whether tape or instruments play (instruments always have conventional notation). Upon even cursory examination, one can see that the notational marks for the electronic part simply approximate graphically the audio sound. For instance, white noise is ▨▨▨ , trill is ⊓⊔⊓⊔⊓ , echo ◗◗◗▶ , a simple sustained one ▬▬▬ . In answer to the question of why the notation at all, it serves as a cue to the conductor. In places where the exact rhythmic configuration is not clearly apparent from the electronic notation, I have put rhythm cues in conventional notation in parenthesis on top of the part.[7]

Dynamics: Dynamics are used in *Spectrum* to create kaleidoscopic effects:

Example 19   Interweaving Dynamics (meas. 121-130)

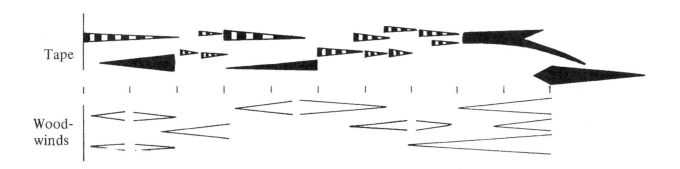

Example 20   Contrasting Dynamics (meas. 38-49)

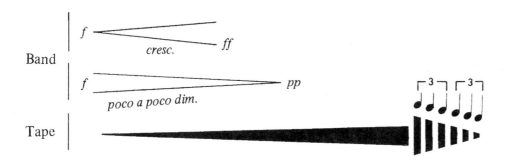

An interesting dynamic effect is achieved just before letter I in the score; here the timpani roll grows out of the fading tape sound and leads into a tutti brass homophonic passage:

Example 21

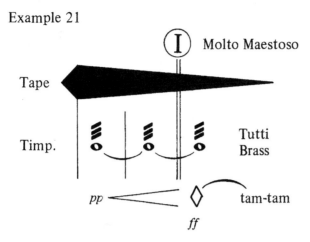

For a clear illustration of the overall dynamic scheme of the work, see the flow chart given at the end of the analytical notes.

Texture: The overall texture in *Spectrum* is, to use the words of the composer, "severely polyphonic." The interweaving of the four musical gestures and their "simultaneous inter-metamorphosis" gives the piece its kaleidoscopic nature, a "polyphony of musical gestures."[8] Other noteworthy textural effects include:

1. a brief contrasting homophonic passage in the brass (letter I)
2. a trio for solo oboe, solo cornet, and tape (letter E)
3. a battle between percussion and tape ostinato (mea. 169)
4. tape *scorrevole* punctuated by tutti band chords (letter J)

Form: The overall form of *Spectrum* is ternary:

Section A: Band alone.

Section B: In two phrases:
1. Tape alone.
2. Begins with tape alone but soon dissolves into a trio for oboe, cornet, and tape, culminating into a complete integration of the band.

Section A_1:   Recapitulation of section A (band alone for some twelve measures); this is followed by a section with tape ostinato and band (includes the battle between the tape and percussion) that moves to a climax three measures from the end. The work ends with a very short coda (tape fade out.)

See the flow chart that follows for details.

Flow Chart: *Spectrum* by Herbert Bielawa

58

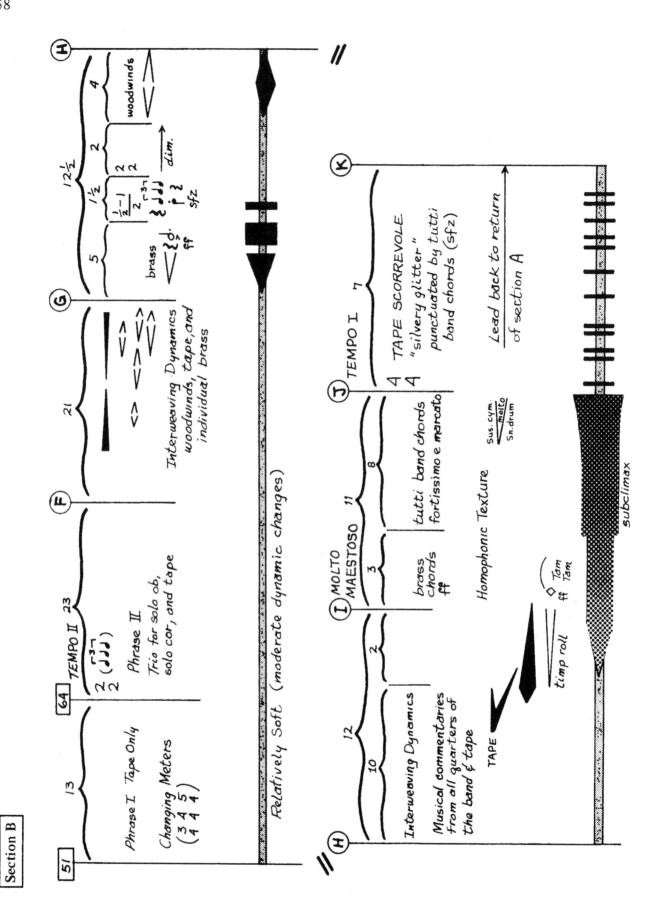

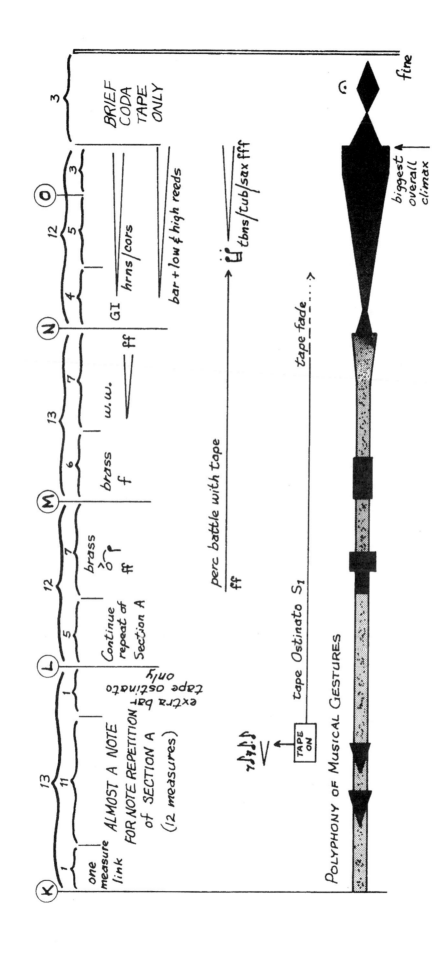

Section A₁

Abbreviated Flow Chart

Overall Form: Ternary

A B A₁

Unit Study Lesson Plan

Spectrum by Herbert Bielawa

Concepts, Subconcepts, and Objectives

Melody Twelve-Tone Row or Series (Original, Inversion, Retrograde, Retrograde Inversion, Transposition, Permutation), Intervals (Major and Minor Seconds—Whole and Half Steps), Musical Gesture, Articulations (Legato, Secco and Tenuto Staccato, and Marcato)

Objectives The student can be expected to:

Transform a given twelve-tone row using standard permutation techniques.

Identify aurally major and minor seconds when given in melodic interval dictation exercises.

Identify aurally and visually the four musical gestures found in *Spectrum.*

Demonstrate through performance an understanding of basic articulations: legato, secco and tenuto staccato, and marcato.

Harmony Tone Clusters, Intervals (Major Seconds and Sevenths, and Tritones), Parallel Interval Doubling (Color Doubling)

Objectives The student can be expected to:

Identify aurally and visually tone cluster sonorities in given musical examples.

Identify aurally and visually parallel major seconds, major sevenths, and tritones in given musical examples.

Rhythm Meter ($\frac{1}{2}$-1), Cross-meter Triplets, Polyrhythms, Syncopation, Disjunct Rhythms

Objectives The student can be expected to:

Demonstrate through performance an understanding of the meter signature ($\frac{1}{2}$-1).

Demonstrate through performance an understanding of cross-meter triplets, polyrhythms, and syncopation.

Identify visually disjunct rhythms in given musical examples.

Perform and notate from dictation given rhythmic patterns, utilizing the following rhythms, rests, and meters:

Bandstration Special Effects (Interval Color Doubling, Muted Tones, Glissando, Extreme Register Scoring, Percussion Effects, Flutter Tongue, Electronically Transformed Sound)

Objectives The student can be expected to:

Identify aurally or visually special bandstration effects when used in given musical examples.

Demonstrate through performance at least three special sound effects playable on the student's own instrument.

Dynamics Interweaving Dynamics, Contrasting Dynamics, Dynamic Accent (Sforzando)

Objectives The student can be expected to:

Demonstrate through performance an understanding of dynamic accent (sfz).

Demonstrate through performance an understanding of contrasting and interweaving dynamics.

Texture Polyphony (Polyphony of Musical Gestures), Homophony

Objectives The student can be expected to:

Identify aurally given passages of music as being either homophonic or polyphonic.

Explain orally or in writing the musical significance of the phrase "polyphony of musical gestures" as it relates to *Spectrum*.

Form Ternary Form (Three-Part)

Objectives The student can be expected to:

Identify aurally or visually ternary form in given compositions.

Describe the distinguishing musical features that differentiate sections in a given three-part form composition.

Additional
    Concepts   Mixed Media, *Musique Concrète,* Electronically Transformed Sounds,
                  White Noise, *Scorrevole,* Tape Ostinato, Graphic Notation, Spectrum
                  (Kaleidoscopic Color Sonorities)

Additional Objectives The student can be expected to:

Identify through aural analysis the performance media of given compositions:
    electronic music, mixed media, band, and orchestra.

Identify through aural analysis the tape manipulation techniques used to transform
    the basic sound sources (piano and white noise) in the work under study.

Identify visually examples of graphic notation in given musical examples.

Appraise orally or in writing the aesthetic qualities in the mixed media work under study.

Glossary of Musical Terms

Coda — (Italian, tail) an added section at the end of a composition.

Consonance and Dissonance — relative terms used to describe the agreeable or disagreeable effects produced
    by intervals, chords, and sounds in general.

Disjunct Rhythm — a disjointed rhythm pattern that does not follow the normal metric scheme.

Electronic Music — electronically generated and transformed sound.

Graphic Notation — unconventional music notation that illustrates in realistic detail the actual sounds
    produced.

Homophony — (homo = same or similar, phony = sound, literally similar sound) a term used to describe
    the texture of a musical composition in which one voice leads melodically with a chordal accompani-
    ment.

Kaleidoscopic — in *Spectrum,* the term refers to the variegated and ever-changing patterns of musical
    sound.

Mixed Media — two or more different performance media. In *Spectrum,* the mixing of prerecorded
    electronic tape and band.

Musical Gesture — in *Spectrum,* a relatively short, self-contained musical idea in a melodic or harmonic
    context.

Musique Concrète — not to be confused with pure electronic music. *Musique concrète* makes use of
    natural everyday sounds that are modified and transformed by tape manipulation techniques and
    electronic treatment.

Ostinato — (Italian, obstinate) a melodic or rhythmic phrase that is repeated persistently throughout a
    composition or section thereof.

Permutation — any reordering of a given set of elements. For example, the notes A B♭ C can be permuted
    as follows: B♭ C A, C A B♭, B♭ A C, C B♭ A, and A C B♭.

Polyphony — (poly = many, phony = sound, the oppsite of homophony) music in which all parts contribute more or less equally to the musical fabric.

Polyphony of Musical Gestures — in *Spectrum,* the inter-metamorphosis of four musical gestures.

Scorrevole (Italian, freely flowing) – in *Spectrum,* the term refers to the extremely high, fast, and freely flowing tape sound that occurs at letter J in the score. These sounds were produced through tape manipulation techniques—increased speed changes.

Serial Composition — a radical system of composition originated by Arnold Schoenberg in an attempt to arrive at a compositional method that would supersede traditional methods of composing based on tonal systems.

Spectrum — used in the title of the work under study to mean a series of sound images.

Syncopation — any deliberate upsetting of the normal meter, pulse, or rhythm by emphasizing weak beats in a measure or weak parts of a beat.

Ternary Form — a general term used to describe the form of a composition that contains three distinct parts: statement, departure, and restatement (ABA).

Tone Cluster — several notes grouped closely together, producing a dissonant chord.

White Noise — sound containing an equal distribution of overtones covering the entire spectrum of frequencies. White noise can be filtered into bands of sound having definite pitch and timbre through electronic manipulation.

Musical Terms from the Score:

maestoso —

molto —

poco a poco —

divisi —

secco —

Activities for Teaching Comprehensive Musicianship

Introduction:
Play a good recorded performance of *Spectrum* before attempting to rehearse the work. Reason: the work is unusual, difficult, and the students need to have a general aural impression of the pre-recorded tape and band parts together. Preface the playing of the recording with a few brief remarks about the composition (see "Historical Notes").

Warm-Up Drills (Skills Development—Aural, Dexterous, and Translative):
Relate warm-up drills to the development of skills needed to perform *Spectrum*—scales (intervals), rhythms, articulations, dynamics, tempos.

1. Distribute the Student Guide for *Spectrum* and assign the skills development material for home practice.

2. Use the same material for warm-up drills each time *Spectrum* is rehearsed. Combine the rhythm patterns given in the Study Guide as follows:

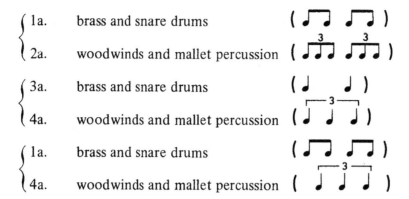

Reverse any or all of the above; other combinations are possible.

Explain "cross-meter triplets" (four against three); conduct the measure in 4/4 time and cut time.

Vary the scale and rhythmic drills by using contrasting dynamics and different tempos. Be sure to use percussion in the warm-up drills—two players on each mallet instrument.

Melodic and Harmonic Tonal Organization:

1. Explain the basic tonal organization of *Spectrum*, using the Student Study Guide. Go over the reading and listening assignment in the Study Guide.

2. Define "musical gesture" (see "Glossary of Musical Terms"), and rehearse separately each of the four musical gestures found in *Spectrum:*

   Gesture I   (horns – beginning) "cross-meter triplets – color motion"

   Gesture II   (fls, obs, vib – beginning) "sustained texturized tones"

   Gesture III   (cors, cls - beginning) "dialogue"

   Gesture IV   (low brass and flutes – meas. 5-7) "broad ejaculatory tone cluster sonorities"

   a. Have the students look through their parts to identify and mark important recurrences of the four musical gestures (G I, G II, G III, G IV).

   b. Illustrate and explain how the composer derived the melodic and harmonic materials used in the four musical gestures from the three-part series.

Suggestion: Use an opaque projector and screen to illustrate the four gestures. Use the musical examples given in the "Analytical Notes" (Examples 2, 3, 4, and 5) or use the score.

G I is derived from series part 3.

G II is derived from series part 2 with G♮ omitted.

G III is derived from series part 1.

G IV is derived from series part 2.

3. Explain and discuss Bielawa's use of dissonant harmonic chord structures, tone clusters.

    Suggestion: Write the tone cluster given in Example 10 ("Analytical Notes") on the chalkboard. Have the low brass and horns sustain the eighth note in measure 11. After analyzing the chord, the students should discover that the sonority contains all notes of the series except D natural.

4. Explain Bielawa's use of dissonant parallel interval doubling. Rehearse separately the following instruments:

—horns and cornets (letter C)	parallel major seconds
—trombones (measure 16)	parallel major sevenths
—horns (beginning)	parallel major sevenths
—cornets (measure 14)	parallel tritone intervals

    Point out that other parallel interval doublings are also used—major sixths, major ninths, and minor sevenths.

    Suggestion: Illustrate examples of parallel intervals on the chalkboard or use an opaque projector to show examples from the score or "Analytical Notes" (Examples 2, 11, and 12).

5. Explain and discuss serial compositional techniques using the information given in the Student Study Guide.

6. Periodically incorporate brief melodic and harmonic dictation exercises into the rehearsals of *Spectrum*. Concentrate on developing student aural discrimination of major and minor second melodic intervals (up and down), and parallel harmonic intervals (major seconds and sevenths, and tritones). For example, play the following exercises at the piano; the students should identify the intervals aurally and respond orally.

Dictation Examples

Melodic Intervals

Harmonic Intervals

M2nds   M7ths   Tritones

Rhythm:

1. Go over the *Practical Procedures for Mastering Complex Rhythmical Passages* and the rhythmic duet homework assignment given in the Student Study Guide.

2. Rehearse and explain the following rhythmical complexities in *Spectrum:*

    a. ½-1 / 2 meter signature (measure 114); use the explanation given in the Analytical Notes.

    b. Polyrhythms (measures 10 and 161). Write the following rhythms on the chalkboard and rehearse each part separately before combining them:

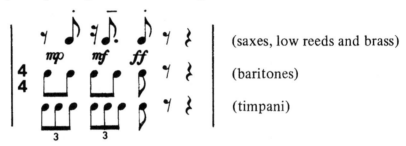

(saxes, low reeds and brass)

(baritones)

(timpani)

    c. Syncopations. Play the following syncopations on a unison concert B^b, then add the given pitches:

Mea. 179 (high brass)

Mea. 181 (high brass and tbns)

Meas. 185-187 (high woodwinds)

    d. Disjunct rhythms (measures 38-46, trombones, tubas, and saxes). Write the following example on the chalkboard and explain disjunct rhythms:

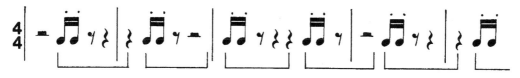

3/4 time implied

Compare measures 38-46 to measures 193-201; note the change in dynamics and different articulations used in the saxophone parts.

    e.   Rehearse other rhythmically complex passages as needed, especially the cross-meter triplets occurring at the beginning and again at letter K. Although written in 4/4 time, the beat pattern may change to 2/2 time in certain measures to accommodate the quarter-note triplets; experimentation is needed to find the best solution to the problem.

3.   Periodically incorporate brief rhythmic dictation exercises into the rehearsals of *Spectrum*. Concentrate on developing aural discrimination of patterns, utilizing the following meters, rhythms, and rests:

Use the rhythmic exercises given in the warm-up drills for dictation materials; add rests at random. If appropriate, use student-composed rhythmic duets for dictation.

Bandstration:

1.   Illustrate (students perform) Bielawa's use of special bandstration effects in *Spectrum;* use examples given in the "Analytical Notes" (see under "Bandstration").

2.   In class, go over the bandstration assignment given in the Student Study Guide.

Dynamics:

Illustrate and discuss Bielawa's use of dynamics to achieve kaleidoscopic effects; use the examples given in the "Analytical Notes" (see under "dynamics"). Be sure to compare measures 38-46 to measures 193-201; the biggest climax is achieved at bar 201, due to a change of dynamics in the saxophone, trombone, and tuba parts.

Texture:

1.   Discuss Bielawa's use of the phrase "polyphony of musical gestures"; refer to the comments given in the "Analytical Notes" under "Texture."

2.   Rehearse the brief homophonic passage at letter I. Point out that this isolated homophonic passage provides needed textural contrast.

Form:

Outline the overall formal scheme of *Spectrum* on the chalkboard; use the outline given in the "Analytical Notes" under "Form." Rehearse each section separately so that the students have a clear understanding of the form, then:

a. Discuss Bielawa's reason for using a straightforward, three-part form in the work (rationale: to counterbalance the nontraditional aspects of the piece—electronic sounds and cluster sonorities).

b. Discuss the importance of ternary form in music:

    statement – contrast – restatement

    exposition – development – recapitulation

    chorus – bridge – chorus

c. Discuss the various ways a composer can vary different sections of a composition to provide variety and contrast. Consider the structural elements: melody, harmony, rhythm, and so on. Use *Spectrum* as a springboard for discussion. Compare other rehearsal compositions if appropriate.

Graphic Notation and Prerecorded Electronic Tape Sounds:

1. Write the following graphic notation symbols on the chalkboard:

white noise   trill

echo   crescendo

glissando   decrescendo

simple sustained tone

    a. Use an opaque projector to illustrate examples of graphic notation from the full score:

        page 11 (symbols given above)

        page 21 tape *scorrevole* (letter J)

        page 25 tape ostinato (letter L, before and after)

    b. Play a recording of these passages while the students follow the score on the screen. Alternative: Play on the prerecorded tape part on a tape recorder.

    c. Initiate a group discussion of Bielawa's use of graphic notation to represent the prerecorded tape sounds and the tape recorder manipulation techniques used to transform the basic sound sources, white noise and piano. Refer to the "Analytical Notes" under "Bandstration."

2. In class, be sure to go over the following terms: white noise, *scorrevole*, ostinato, *musique concrète,* and mixed media. See the "Glossary of Musical Terms" for concise definitions.

3. Explain and discuss tape recorder manipulation techniques used in *Spectrum:*

a. tape cutting and splicing

b. speed changes—fast, slow, speeding up or slowing down—all cause frequency changes; note the extremely fast speed used to produce the tape *scorrevole* at letter J (the "silvery glitter" sounds are two octaves above the piccolo and piano range)

c. echo feedback—echo effects

d. gain control—crescendos and decrescendos

e. reverse taping—retrograde

f. tape loop—used to produce the ostinato before and after letter L. Bracket the recurring five-note group in the score before illustrating the passage on the screen; explain that the five-note group is derived from part one of the series, and that the ostinato is disjunct with the bar lines.

4. Questions for discussion:

Why did the composer use unorthodox notation?

Is the notation a fairly accurate graphic representation of what you hear?

Comments on the notation:
Notational systems are similar to written language systems in that both are symbolic representations of something communicative. Many systems have been devised for notating music in different historical periods. Music notation systems have evolved like language systems.

Conventional music notation used during the past 300 years is no longer adequate for contemporary composers of electronic and other avant-garde music. Many contemporary composers are creating their own notational systems to better represent and communicate their musical ideas.

5. Optional Activities:

a. Encourage the band members to bring in examples of music that illustrate unconventional notational systems, either old or new. Assign one student to arrange a bulletin board display of the materials (acceptable as a band project).

b. Invite an electronic music composer into the school to demonstrate the techniques of transforming sound with the use of a tape recorder.

c. Encourage the band members to compose a short piece using tape recorder manipulation techniques to transform conventional sound sources (acceptable as a band project).

d. Encourage the band members to bring in their own recordings of electronic music or *musique concrète*. Set aside one rehearsal period for listening to and discussing these works. Let the students introduce their own recordings.

Performance Aspects:

1. Comment on the interpretive aspects of the work (see "Historical Notes" under "Performance and Interpretive Aspects of the Work").

2. Rehearse the following passages separately with interpretive comments:

    a. letter E (a trio for solo oboe, solo cornet, and tape—balance parts)

    b. letter J (tape *scorrevole*—"silvery glitter"—punctuated by tutti band chords)

    c. measures 169-176 (battle between the percussion and an arrogant tape ostinato—percussion tries to overpower the tape)

    > Question: How does the composer achieve the effect of a battle between the tape and percussion?

    > Answer: Through rhythmic, dynamic, and harmonic (brass chords) tension. Compare the contrasting middle section (phrase II-trio for oboe, cornet, and tape); note here that the instruments are in agreement with the tape.

Aesthetics:

1. Stimulate a group discussion concerning the aesthetic qualities in *Spectrum*. Sample questions:

    Do you like *Spectrum?* Why?

    Can you describe the unique musical features in the work?

    Discuss the musical significance of the words "spectrum" and "kaleidoscopic color sonorities" as they relate to the composition.

    How can you tell that *Spectrum* was written in the twentieth century and not in the nineteenth century?

    In your opinion, is *Spectrum* a mediocre, good, or excellent composition? Why? Consider whether or not the composer had anything to say musically. Was he convincing in saying what he had to say? Was it worth saying?

2. Optional Activities:

    a. Field Trip: Visit an electronic studio at a local university for a demonstration and lecture on electronic music.

    b. Performance Suggestion: Include a kaleidoscopic light show or slide projections of contemporary art with the concert performance of *Spectrum*.

Terminology:

1. Assign two students the task of looking up musical terms from the score given in the Glossary. Definitions are to be given orally in class.

2. Go over all definitions given in the Glossary before the final unit evaluation to be sure each student understands the terms.

Evaluation:

Set aside one band period to give the final unit examination.

Final Unit Examination

1. Write a brief definition of at least four of the following musical terms:

   a. tone cluster   f. electronic music

   b. mixed media   g. ostinato

   c. *musique concrète*   h. *scorrevole*

   d. white noise   i. serial music

   e. graphic notation

2. Listen to the following recorded excerpts of contemporary musical works and:

   a. Identify the performance medium—band, band and prerecorded tape (mixed), orchestra, orchestra and prerecorded tape (mixed), or pure electronic music.

   b. If prerecorded tape sounds are included in the example, identify the basic sound sources—white noise, conventional instruments, human voices, electronically generated sounds, others.

   Suggestion: Play two or three short excerpts from the following list of recorded compositions:

   Meditation by Gunther Schuller
        Educational Record Reference Library, Number 24
        Performance Medium: band
        Example: twelve-tone serial music

   Gesang der Jünglinge (Song of the Youths) by Karlheinz Stockhausen
        Deutsche Grammophon Gesellschaft SLPM 138811
        Performance Medium: prerecorded electronic tape
        Example: *musique concrete,* combines children's voices and electronically
            produced sound

   A Piece for Tape Recording by Vladimir Ussachevsky
        Composers Recordings Inc. CRI — 112
        Performance Medium: prerecorded electronic tape
        Example: electronically generated and transformed sounds

   Poème Électronique by Edgard Varèse
        Columbia Records MS 6146 or ML 5478
        Performance Medium: prerecorded tape

Example: *musique concrète* combines electronically generated and transformed sound with bells and the human voice

Rhapsodic Variations for Tape Recorder and Orchestra by Otto Luening and Vladimir Ussachevsky
Louisville Orchestra First Edition Records, 1954, Part Two
Performance Medium: orchestra and prerecorded tape (mixed)
Example: *musique concrète,* the prerecorded tape part utilizes instrumental sound sources that have been transformed electronically

3. Listen to the following recorded performance of *Stargazing* by Donald Erb and:

a. Identify the performance medium.

b. Construct a flow chart of what you hear for each of the three short movements.

c. Summarize your findings by discussing the structural elements of the work, especially the melodic, harmonic, rhythmic, bandstration, and textural elements.

Suggestion: Play all three short movements of the work at least two times.

Stargazing by Donald Erb   I. The Stars Come Out   II. Comets, Meteors, Shooting Stars
III. The Surface of the Sun

Educational Record Reference Library, Number 26
Performance Medium: band and prerecorded electronic tape (mixed)

Possible comments on the structural elements:

Movement I:	free rhythm, quasi-aleatoric, pointillistic, piano effects (plucking and strumming on the strings), density crescendo, special percussion effects
Movement II:	chromatic scale passages (woodwinds), slide whistles, brass and woodwind trills and glissandi, quasi-contrapuntal textures
Movement III:	tone cluster chords, flutter tonguing, extreme register scoring, membrane percussion effects, homophonic texture with a continuous undertone (pedal point)

Student Study Guide

Unit Study Composition: *Spectrum* by Herbert Bielawa

Contents[9]

Concepts, Subconcepts, and Objectives

Glossary of Musical Terms

Activities, Resources, and Assignments with Options

Evaluation

Summary of Assignments	Check List
Practice Assignment	————
Reading and Listening Assignment	————
Composition Assignments:	
Twelve-Tone Row	————
Rhythmic Duets	————
Special Effects (Bandstration)	————
Optional Assignments (Band Projects)	————

Activities, Resources, and Assignments With Options

Skills Development Material

Assignment: Practice the following scales, rhythms, and articulations daily. Start slowly at first and gradually increase your speed.

Whole Tone Scales: Whole tone scales are constructed in a series of six whole tones. A whole tone or step, usually written as a major second interval, equals two half steps. There are only two different whole tone scales. Splitting a whole tone scale down the middle produces two tritone intervals; a tritone interval equals three whole tones.

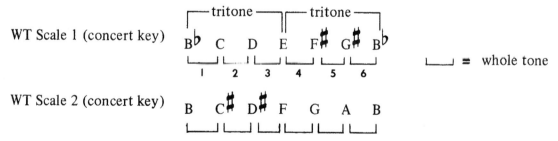

Chromatic Scales: A chromatic scale is constructed in a series of twelve half steps. A half step, sometimes written as a minor second, is the smallest possible interval in the equal-tempered scale.

Chromatic Scale (concert key)

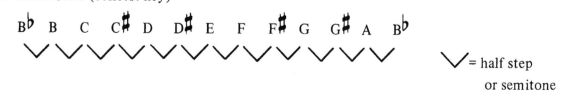

Transposing instruments use the following scales:

B♭ Transposing Instruments (B♭ cl, bass cl, ten sax, trp, 𝄞 bar):

WT Scale 1	C	D	E	F♯	G♯	A♯	C
WT Scale 2	C♯	D♯	F	G	A	B	C♯

Chromatic Scale C C♯ D D♯ E F F♯ G G♯ A A♯ B C

E♭ Transposing Instruments (E♭ sop cl, alto cl, alto and bar sax):

WT Scale 1	G	A	B	C♯	D♯	F	G
WT Scale 2	G♯	A♯	C	D	E	F♯	G♯

Chromatic Scale G G♯ A A♯ B C C♯ D D♯ E F F♯ G

F Transposing Instrument (Fr hrn, Eng hrn):

WT Scale 1	F	G	A	B	C♯	D♯	F
WT Scale 2	F♯	G♯	A♯	C	D	E	F♯

Chromatic Scale F F♯ G G♯ A A♯ B C C♯ D D♯ E F

Rhythms: Vary the scale patterns given above by using the following rhythmic patterns. Repeat the patterns on each degree of the scale.

Articulations: Vary the scale patterns and rhythms using the following articulations:

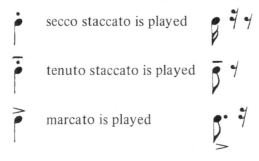

secco staccato is played

tenuto staccato is played

marcato is played

legato is played smoothly (slurred)

sforzando is played with a strong accent;
use an explosive attack (dynamic accent)

sfz

Tonal Organization

Spectrum is tonally organized by the following three-part series:

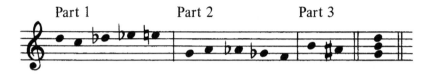

The first two parts of the series contain five notes each, the second part being the exact mirror inversion of the first part at the interval of a fifth. The third part of the series contains two notes a semitone apart. All three parts of the series are constructed in whole and half step intervals. The twelve-tone row or series provides all of the basic melodic and harmonic materials used in the construction of *Spectrum* (band and prerecorded tape parts). Although the harmonic structures of *Spectrum* are nontertial, an interesting thing occurs when you vertically stack the first note of each of the three parts of the series: a G major triad in root position!

Reading and Listening Assignment:

Read the prepared analytical and historical notes for *Spectrum* and listen to the recording of the work while following the score. Notes, scores, and recordings are on reserve in the school library. The assignment should be completed within the next two weeks.

Optional Listening Assignment (acceptable as a band project):

Listen to a selected recording or live performance of at least one of the following compositional types: twelve-tone, serial, electronic music, or *musique concrète,* and write a brief critique about the composition. Consult the record catalogue in the school library–Arnold Schoenberg, Otto Luening, Vladimir Ussachevsky, Karlheinz Stockhausen, Edgard Varèse, and others.

Serial Composition: Serial composition is a twentieth-century system of composing in which a given series of pitches, later to include dynamics, rhythms, timbres–total serialization–provides the tonal basis of a musical composition. The system was devised by the Viennese composer and theorist Arnold Schoenberg (1874-1951) in the 1920s; he called his system a "method of composing with twelve tones which are related only with one another," the so-called twelve-tone technique. The principles of this technique are as follows:

1.   Every composition is based on a specific arrangement of the twelve chromatic tones called a tone row or series.

2.   Theoretically, the chosen succession of tones remains unchanged throughout the composition with one exception–the octave position of any tone of the series may be changed.

3. In addition to the original tone row (0), sometimes called the prime (P), the series may be transformed as follows: (I) inversion—inverted form or mirror, (R) retrograde—reverse order, and (RI) retrograde inversion—reverse order of the inverted form. See the examples below.

4. The four forms of the row may be transposed to any step of the chromatic scale—four forms times twelve possible transpositions equals forty-eight transformations or permutations available.

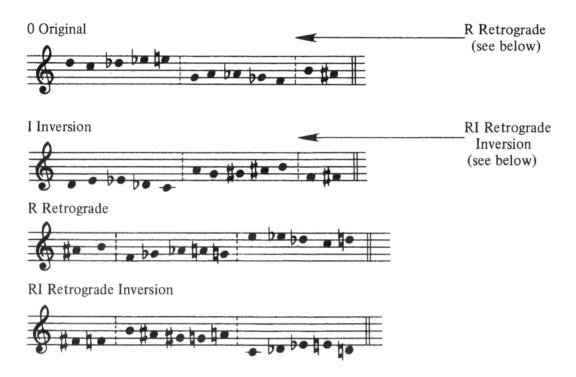

0 Original

R Retrograde (see below)

I Inversion

RI Retrograde Inversion (see below)

R Retrograde

RI Retrograde Inversion

Assignment (to be handed in):

1. Compose your own twelve-tone row. Transform the row using standard permutation techniques. Create a melody for your own instrument out of your original row by adding rhythms, meter and tempo indications, phrasing, articulations, and dynamics.

2. Compose a countermelody to your tone row, using one of the permutated forms. *Alternate:* Compose a harmonic chordal accompaniment to your tone row melody, using chords derived from any of the permutations of the original row.

Optional Assignment (acceptable as a band project):

1. Compose a short but complete musical composition based on your own tone row and its permutations. Score the work for a chamber ensemble of your choice. Rehearse and perform the work in class or in public.

2. Research and prepare a brief written and oral report on any of the following topics: twelve-tone composition, *musique concrète*, the contributions of Arnold Schoenberg, electronic music

3.   Prepare and perform a serial chamber music composition of your choice and write a brief analysis of the work. The performance may be given before the class or in public.

Practical Procedures for Mastering Complex Rhythmical Passages

There are many rhythmical complexities in *Spectrum* that contribute to its kaleidoscopic musical effect. Apply the procedures outlined below and work out the rhythmical difficulties you are encountering in your own part.

1.   Mark in the beats and subdivisions of beats using arrows ↓↑↓↑

2.   Solve the rhythm problem first by omitting ties, articulations, dynamics, and pitch changes. Practice the rhythms slowly at first on any middle register note. Once the rhythms are understood and can be performed accurately, gradually add the other elements—pitches first, then dynamics, articulations and ties. Work up to speed.

3.   If a complex rhythmical passage utilizes variations of either the threefold (♩♩) or fourfold (♫♫) division of the beat, it is sometimes helpful to practice all parts of the beat division first to get a feel for the rhythm:

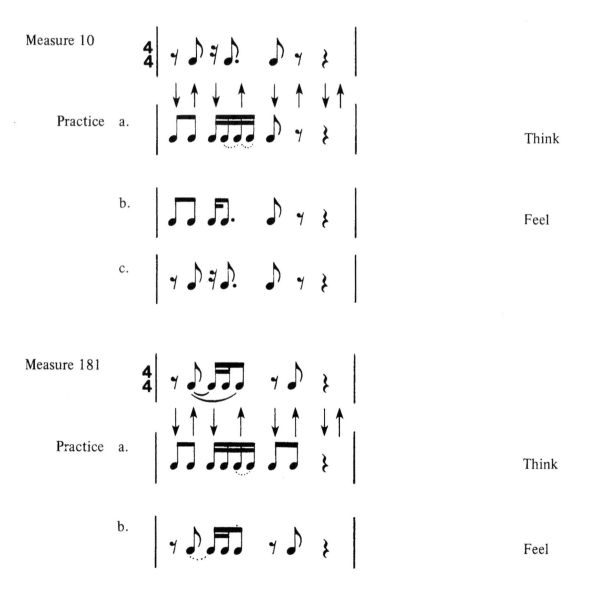

78

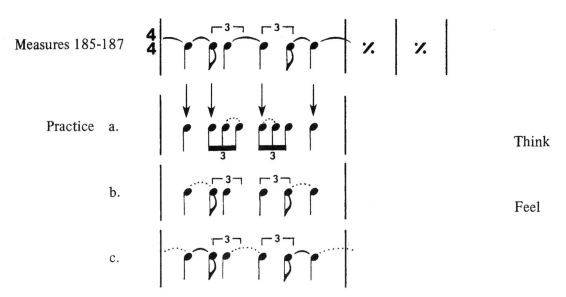

Measures 185-187

Practice a.

Think

b.

Feel

c.

Assignment (to be handed in):

Compose and be able to perform, that is, clap, speak, and play on your instrument, at least two different rhythmic duets using the following rhythms, rests, and meters:

Each duet should contain at least two or more different rhythms and rests and be approximately four to eight measures long.

Format: Rhythmic Duet 1

Part A

Part B

Bandstration

Assignment (to be handed in):

Experiment with the sound of possibilities of your instrument. Try to produce as many different and unusual sound effects as you can. Keep a detailed list of the sound effects you can produce. Be prepared to demonstrate your sound creations in class. Examples:

Playing on a partially assembled instrument.

Playing a brass instrument with a woodwind mouthpiece, or vice versa.

Producing a glissando effect by playing on the head joint of a flute with the index finger inserted in and out of the open end.

Playing on the mouthpiece alone.

Popping the keys on a flute or saxophone without blowing through the instrument.

Holding a drumstick or set of keys against a vibrating tam-tam.

Playing on the rim, shell, or bowl of a percussion instrument.

Optional Assignment (acceptable as a band project):
Invent your own notational symbols to represent the sound creations you have discovered. Compose a short duet, trio, or quartet for like instruments, using your newly discovered sound effects and notational system. Be sure to include an explanation sheet for the unconventional notation. Rehearse and perform the work in class or in public.

Evaluation
There will be a written and listening examination at the end of the study unit. Be sure to review all definitions given in the Glossary of Musical Terms. All out of class assignments should be completed before the final exam. Unit study time: approximately five weeks.

(Upon completion of the study unit insert this guide in your source/reference notebook)

Footnotes (Chapter Four)

[1] Herbert Bielawa, "Spectrum," *Journal of Band Research* (Autumn 1967) Volume IV, Number 1, pp. 12-16.

[2] *Ibid.*, p. 12.

[3] Notes included in the score.

[4] Bielawa, *op. cit.*, p. 12.

[5] *Ibid.*, p. 15.

[6] *Ibid.*, p. 16.

[7] *Ibid.*, p. 16.

[8] *Ibid.*, pp. 12-13.

[9] The Student Study Guide should also include the list of Concepts, Subconcepts, and Objectives, and the Glossary of Musical Terms as given in the Lesson Plan. They were not included here to conserve space.

CHAPTER FIVE

THE SPECIAL STUDY UNIT

Up to this point, the book has covered the framework of the curriculum, organizational and teaching/learning strategies, and the unit study composition. This chapter covers the special study unit and presents three model study unit learning guides: "Basic Conducting for the Student Instrumentalist," "Brass Instrument Transposition and Scoring," and "Acoustics, Tuning and Intonation." In addition, the student learning material for the special study unit on sight reading, "Six Commandments for Developing Sight Reading Skill," is given.

In Chapter One, the special study unit was described as a supplementary instructional unit used to cover a wide range of band-related topics. These topics are "supplementary" only in that they are not directly related to a specific rehearsal/performance composition. The adjective should not be construed to mean "of minor importance." Generally, the special study unit is included in the curriculum to provide students with a basic floor of knowledge and skills.

Several of the special study unit topics suggested below are best taught in beginning band, intermediate band, or in small chamber ensemble classes. Others are best taught in the large performing ensemble in concentrated periods of time when performance is not pressing. Some special study units should be offered in cycles of instruction, that is, once every three or four years or once every other year; others should be offered every year. Suggestions for including the special study unit in the curriculum are given below by topic area.

Basic Conducting: The dexterous skill of conducting should be taught in the curriculum at least once every three or four years. This procedure will guarantee each bandsman the opportunity to conduct the ensemble at least once during his tenure in the program. See the student learning guide for this unit, given on page 83.

Transposition and Scoring: There are several ways to include a study unit on transposition and scoring in the curriculum. You can, for example, cover a different family of instruments each year of a three-year cycle—brass instruments the first year, woodwind instruments the second year, and percussion the third year. In a four-year cycle, the woodwinds can be divided into two groups and covered separately, (1) clarinet choir, and (2) double reeds, saxophones, flutes and piccolo. Another cyclical pattern would alternate a unit on conducting with a unit on transposition and scoring:

First Year — Brass and Percussion Instrument Transposition and Scoring

Second Year — Basic Conducting

Third Year — Woodwind Instrument Transposition and Scoring

Fourth Year — Basic Conducting

Other cyclical patterns are possible. Each band director should select the pattern that best fits his teaching situation. See the student learning guide for this unit, given on page 85.

Acoustics, Tuning, and Intonation: Because of the persistent and sometimes frustrating problem of trying to correct faulty intonation in school band performance, the subject of acoustics, tuning, and intonation should be taught at least once a year as a special introductory study unit. The student learning guide for this unit, given on page 86, can be used as introductory material for new bandsmen and review material for established bandsmen. The subject of acoustics, the science of sound, is included in this study unit because it is pertinent in a fundamental way to developing an understanding of tuning and intonation. Obviously, the concepts to be developed must be limited in scope and depth. Nonetheless, all students need to know and understand a few simple facts concerning the nature of musical sound. From this writer's experience, it has been shown that some science-oriented band students become so intrigued by the acoustics of music that learning is extended way beyond the established objectives for the study unit.

Sight Reading: The translative skill of sight reading is best taught in concentrated periods of time at least two or three times a year—early in the fall to determine ensemble's skill level, midyear to prepare for the sight reading festival, and in the late spring to evaluate progress.[1] A student learning guide need not be developed for this study unit. All the student needs is a copy of the "Six Commandments for Developing Sight Reading Skill" given on page 88. The commandments should be reproduced in the form of a large wall chart for display in the rehearsal hall. Every time a composition is to be played for the first time, refer to the commandments, especially numbers three, four, and six. In ensemble sight reading, the approach should be similar to that used at sight reading festivals. First, allow your students a few minutes to silently analyze the music following the analytical guide given in commandment number six. Second, "walk through" the composition with the students, pointing out typical problems to watch out for: meter and tempo changes, key changes, climaxes, repeat signs, and so on. Next, sight-read straight through the piece without stopping, if at all possible. After sight reading through the piece, ask your students to analyze their own mistakes to determine which category of problems needs special work.

Fundamentals of Music: The fundamentals of music should be covered each year as a series of mini-study units for new students entering the program. These units should be correlated with the fundamentals of technique in the beginning or intermediate band. The raw material for these mini-units should be included in the source/reference notebook. The material should cover:

> The Keyboard, Great Staff, and Clefs
>
> Scale Types and Patterns
>
> Intervals
>
> Key Cycle and Key Signatures
>
> Chord Types
>
> Meters
>
> Note Values and Rests
>
> Rhythm Patterns

All novice bandsmen will need to acquire basic concepts and skills related to this material if they are to respond intelligently to comprehensive musicianship instruction that will be offered later on through the rehearsal/performance literature, particularly instruction dealing with the structure of music: melody, harmony, and rhythm. Consider, for example, the importance of intervals in music: (1) scales and chords are constructed with intervals, (2) both the horizontal and vertical organization of pitches in music are composed of intervals, (3) instrument transposition requires a working knowledge of intervals, and (4) twelve-tone permutation techniques deal with intervals. The student who has not been taught to play, sing, hear, write, and visually recognize intervals is going to be severely handicapped in his ability to respond to comprehensive musicianship instruction, and hence, to grow musically.

Common Musical Terms: This special study unit should be covered once a year in the beginning or intermediate band. New bandsmen need a working vocabulary to function effectively in a large performing ensemble. The teaching material for this study unit should be included in the Source/Reference Notebook. See Appendix A under "Glossary of Common Musical Terms and Symbols."

Instrument Care and Maintenance: As with the previous topic, this special study unit should be covered once a year for new bandsmen entering the program. To facilitate the instructional process and to help avoid the endless repetition of instructions and reminders pertaining to the care and maintenance of instruments, it is recommended that the band director purchase multiple copies of the Preventive Mainten-ance[2] pamphlets written by Otto H. Weisshaar. These pamphlets are excellent instructional guides for the proper care and maintenance of instruments.

The following section of this chapter presents three student learning guides and the "Six Commandments for Developing Sight Reading Skill." The resource material that would normally be included in the learning guides is omitted. Instead, a general description of the material is given. With little or no modification, these models can be adapted for use in almost any junior or senior high school band program.

Student Learning Guide 1: Basic Conducting for the Student Instrumentalist[3]

Rationale: To perform effectively in a large performing ensemble, you must learn how to read and respond to the conductor's baton technique. This presupposes an understanding of beat patterns and styles, preparatory gestures, cueing, dynamic gestures, cutoffs, and subdivision. The best way to acquire an understanding of conducting gestures is through practical conducting experience. This study unit, therefore, is designed to introduce you to the technique of conducting and to help you develop basic conducting skills. Two major goals are: (1) to increase your understanding of and responsiveness to the conductor's baton, and (2) to identify talented student conductors who can assist the director by conducting rehearsals, sectionals, and concerts.

Objectives: You will be expected to

Demonstrate an understanding of beat patterns by conducting 2/4, 3/4, 4/4, and 6/8 time, using the dead gesture and the espressivo legato style.

Optional: Do same for light staccato and marcato styles.

Demonstrate the technique of conducting preparatory beats and cutoffs through given conducting examples.

Demonstrate two ways to achieve a crescendo while conducting.

Demonstrate two ways to cue an entrance while conducting.

Demonstrate the correct way to conduct subdivided beats in 2/4, 3/4, 4/4 time, using the dead gesture and espressivo legato beat style.

Conduct a short musical selection in front of a group of student musicians, using proper techniques: preparatory gestures, beat patterns and styles, cueing, and cutoffs.

Activities, Resources, and Assignments With Options:

1. Study the resource material included in the learning guide and practice the exercises until you can demonstrate your proficiency.

2. Conduct the ensemble in class, using music from *Fifty Chorales for Band*[4] by Bill Laas, numbers 40, 44, 47, and 17. Select one or two pieces.

Optional Activities (acceptable as a band project):

   a. Select a piece of music, organize a chamber ensemble, and rehearse and conduct the group in class or in public.

   b. Attend a concert and write a critique on the technique and musical effectiveness of the conductor. Use the conducting evaluation sheet given in your source/reference notebook.

Evaluation: Evaluation will be based on your demonstrated understanding and skill as stated in the objectives and as revealed through: (1) practical conducting work in class, and (2) a written quiz to be given at the end of the study unit.

   (Upon completion of the study unit, insert this learning guide in your source/reference notebook)

Resource Material

The resource material for this learning guide includes diagrams, descriptions, and practice exercises for the following:

   A. *Beat Patterns* — 2/4, 3/4, 4/4, and 6/8 time signatures.
   B. *Beat Styles* — dead gesture, legato, staccato and marcato.
   C. *Preparatory Gestures*
   D. *Conducting Dynamics*
   E. *Cueing*
   F. *Subdivided Beats*
   G. *Cutoffs*
   H. *Fermatas*

Student Learning Guide 2: Brass Instrument Transposition and Scoring

Rationale: This study unit is included in the band curriculum to help you: (1) understand the transposition of your instrument so that you can function effectively in a large performing group; (2) read and translate a transposed score so that you can complete conducting and score study assignments; and (3) acquire skill at transposition and scoring so that you can explore the fields of arranging and composition.

Objectives: You will be expected to

Identify orally or in writing the intervals of transposition for a given list of brass instruments.

Explain orally or in writing why brass instruments transpose.

Identify orally or in writing the written ranges for a given list of brass instruments.

Transpose into concert pitch given examples of written brass parts.

Score a simple four-part chorale or hymn for a given list of brass instruments.

Optional: Arrange a short musical selection for brass instruments.

Activities, Resources, and Assignments With Options:

1. Study the resource material included in this learning guide:
    - I. General Information
    - II. Ranges and Transpositions of Brass Instruments

2. Study the Brass Instrument Relationships and Transposition Reference Charts given in your source/reference notebook.

3. Complete and turn in to your instructor all worksheet assignments included in this learning guide.

    Optional Assignments (acceptable as a band project):

    a. Arrange a short selection of your choosing for brass instruments.

    b. Score your own original composition for brass instruments and perform the work in class or in public.

Evaluation: Evaluation will be based on your demonstrated understanding and skill as stated in the objectives and as revealed through: (1) the homework assignments, (2) an oral quiz to be given in class, (3) applied conducting work in class, and (4) a written examination to be given at the end of the study unit.

(Upon completion of the study unit, insert this learning guide in your source/reference notebook)

Resource Material

The resource material for this learning guide is in two sections:

Section I contains general information on the subject: a brief list of definitions, rules for transposing, score layouts, and answers to the question: why do instruments transpose?

Section II contains the ranges and transpositions of brass instruments and three worksheets for developing skill at transposing.

Student Learning Guide 3: Acoustics, Tuning, and Intonation

Rationale: The ability to play in tune is a musicianly skill that must be developed by every student instrumentalist. The skill involves careful listening and the ability to adjust pitches quickly while playing. Careful listening presupposes a knowledge of what to listen for. The ability to adjust pitches while playing presupposes a knowledge of the skills involved and an understanding of the intonation deficiencies and tendencies of your own instrument. This study unit, therefore, is designed to: (1) introduce you to the fascinating subject of acoustics, tuning, and intonations; (2) sensitize you to the myriad factors that can cause poor intonation; and (3) stimulate in you an ongoing, self-study of the subject with the goal of improving your own intonation.

Objectives: You will be expected to:

Identify orally or in writing a given list of acoustical and musical terms related to the unit topic under study.

Identify orally or in writing at least a half dozen general factors that can cause poor intonation.

Identify orally or in writing typical intonation deficiencies and tendencies of your own instrument.

Demonstrate the correct procedures for tuning your own instrument.

Demonstrate through performance the appropriate techniques for humoring pitches upward or downward when playing.

Demonstrate an understanding of the chromatic stroboscope by using this device for intonation charting and tuning of your own instrument.

Activities, Resources, and Assignments With Options:

1. Study the resource material included in this learning guide:

    I.   Glossary of Acoustical and Musical Terms
    II. Factors That Can Cause Poor Intonation
    III. Inherent Intonation Deficiencies of Wind and Percussion Instruments
    IV. Summary of "Techniques for Humoring Pitches" and "Intonation Flaws" for Each Instrument

2. Study the tuning guide for your instrument that is in your music folder.[5] Be sure you can demonstrate the tuning procedures outlined in the guide.

3. View a film titled the *Nature of Sound* in the media center.[6] Check with the librarian for viewing times.

4. Study the "Instrument Relationships Chart" that is hanging on the wall in the rehearsal hall for your instrument family. The chart contains additional information on the acoustical characteristics of your instrument.[7]

5. *Out of class assignment:* Chart the intonation of your instrument using the "Guide for Charting Intonation Discrepancies With the Strob"; ask your instructor for a copy. Charting procedures and use of the stroboscope will be demonstrated in class. The completed chart must be turned in to your instructor by the end of the study unit, approximately two weeks. Established members of the ensemble must rechart their intonation to see if any progress has been made since last year.

    Optional Activities (acceptable as a band project):

    a. Listen to *The Science of Sound,* a documentary produced by the Bell Telephone Laboratories Incorporated,[8] and write a brief report on the contents. The two-record volume is on reserve in the media center.

    b. Design and construct a simple wind, percussion, or string instrument and demonstrate the instrument in class.

    c. Read a book of your choice related to the topic of this study unit and write a book report. Alternative: Read three articles and write brief resumes of the contents. Consult the source/reference notebook for format outlines. Topics may include: the acoustics of music or musical instruments; the history of musical instruments; or the selection, care, and maintenance of musical instruments.

    d. Interview at least two competent performing musicians who play the instrument you play, and write a report. Questions should focus specifically on the intonation deficiencies and tendencies of the instrument and the techniques used to correct intonation flaws.

Evaluation: Evaluation will be based upon your demonstrated knowledge, understanding, and skill, as stated in the objectives and as revealed through: (1) a written examination to be given at the end of the study unit, (2) an oral quiz to be given in class, and (3) the out-of-class intonation charting assignment.

(Upon completion of the study unit, insert this learning guide in your source/reference notebook)

Resource Material

The resource material for this learning guide is comprehensive in scope because the subject matter is complex.

Section I contains definitions for more than a dozen acoustical and musical terms, some with illustrations.

Section II outlines in six categories the myriad factors that can cause poor intonation.

Section III covers the inherent intonation deficiencies of brass, woodwind, and percussion instruments.

Section IV summarizes the techniques for humoring pitches and intonation flaws for each instrument.

Student Learning Material: Six Commandments for Developing Sight Reading Skill

Rationale: The ability to read music at sight with good musicianship is a necessary and important skill for every school bandsman to develop. If you have not developed your sight reading skill along with other skills, you will be a handicapped musician. At one time or another you will be called upon to sight-read unfamiliar music. Sight reading is a normal part of auditions that are routine for getting into school groups, county and state bands, community groups, military bands, music schools, and conservatories. In addition, you will frequently have to read new music in school ensemble rehearsals. Lacking the skill to be in control of these situations can be frustrating and sometimes demoralizing. The goal, then, is to help you develop skill and confidence in being able to read music fairly accurately the first time around. Highly developed sight reading skill is one mark of an accomplished musician—"show me a good sight reader and I will show you a fine performer."

1. *Sight Read More:* "We learn by doing." Set aside a specific part of *each* practice period (lesson or rehearsal) for sight reading practice. Just as you work to develop and improve your tone quality, intonation, and technical skill, so it is with sight reading. Sight-read the best of the old as well as the new. If you have difficulty sight reading music, start with easy material first. As your skill begins to improve, gradually increase the difficulty of the material.

2. *Develop the Proper Attitude:* "A strong desire to become an excellent sight reader." Become a *first-time* sight reader, not a second- or third-time sight reader. Every new piece of music encountered in a rehearsal should be viewed as an opportunity for developing your sight reading skill.

3. *Develop Your Powers of Concentration:* "A question of mind over matter." Reading music at sight requires *total* concentration. Practice sight reading when your mind is fresh and alert.

4. ***Don't Stop:*** "Good sight readers are constantly reading ahead." When you sight-read a piece of music, don't stop until you reach the end. In ensemble sight reading, always try to keep your place in the music by focusing on beat one in each measure; skip what is too difficult and come back in when you can.

5. ***Know Your Instrument:*** "Good sight readers recognize patterns of sounds and rhythms." Technical proficiency on your instrument is necessary if you wish to become a good sight reader— scales, arpeggios, intervals, articulations, dynamic control, range, flexibility, tone, phrasing, alternate fingerings or slide positions, and so on.

6. ***Analyze the Music Before Playing It:*** "Sight-read it in your head before you sight-play it on your instrument." The translation of music symbols into musical sounds at sight is a complicated skill of a very high order. The skill can be developed if the problems involved are analyzed and dealt with systematically. The problems fall into four broad categories: rhythm problems, pitch problems, problems dealing with style and expression, and miscellaneous problems. Before sight reading a new piece of music, each category should be mentally analyzed with instrument in hand as outlined below. Always work from the general to the specific.

Analytical Guide for Sight Reading

Rhythm:

a. Overall tempo indications, including variations and changes of tempo.

b. Time signatures, especially changes of time signatures that alter the basic pulse unit, for example, 4/4 to 3/2.

c. Specific rhythm problems—dotted and tied notes, triplets, syncopation, juxtaposition of diverse rhythm groups, unusually slow or fast rhythms, complicated combinations of rhythms and rests, and so on.

Pitch:

a. Overall tonality, harmonic base, or pitch center(s).

b. Key signatures and changes of key (including modulations).

c. Specific pitch problems—difficult or unusual intervals, arpeggios, scale passages, and accidentals that interrupt the flow of the line.

Style and Expression:

a. General style or spirit of the music (scherzando, marziale, cantabile).

b. Articulations (staccato, marcato, legato, tenuto).

c. Dynamics and phrasing.

d. Embellishments (trills, mordents, turns, appoggiaturas, grace notes).

Miscellaneous:

a. Special effects (mutes, flutter tongue).

b. Repeat signs, first and second endings, da capo (D. C.), dal segno (D.S. 𝄋), and coda (𝄌) signs.

c. Railroad tracks (//), fermatas (𝄐), and grand pauses (G.P.).

(Upon completion of the study unit, insert this learning material in your source/reference notebook)

Footnotes (Chapter Five)

[1] The Watkins-Farnum Performance Scale (Hall Leonard Music, Inc., 64 East 2nd Street, Winona, Minnesota) is the only objective sight reading test currently available. It can be used to determine skill levels and to evaluate progress.

[2] Belwin-Mills Publishing Corporation. Individual instrument pamphlets are available for Flute and Piccolo, Clarinet, Oboe, Bassoon, Saxophone, Piston Valve Instruments, Rotary Valve Instruments, Trombone, and Percussion.

[3] This learning guide was developed at the suggestion of a second chair flute player who wanted to learn how to conduct.

[4] Belwin-Mills Publishing Corporation, 1957.

[5] Individual instrument tuning guides are published in *Rehearsal Handbook for Band and Orchestra Students* by Robert Garofalo (listed in Appendix B).

[6] Coronet Instructional Films, Coronet Building, 65 East South Water Street, Chicago, Illinois 60601. This learning guide was written for use in a continuous progress high school. If your school does not have a media center, show the film in class.

[7] The charts, written by the author, may be ordered from The Instrumentalist Company (1418 Lake Street, Evanston, Illinois 60204). For suggestions on how to use the charts as teaching/learning tools, see: "Using Visual Aids to Teach the Acoustical Principles of Brass Instruments," *The Instrumentalist* (November 1969) Volume XXIV, Number 4, pp. 77-79; and "Woodwind Instrument Relationships," *The Instrumentalist* (September 1972) Volume XXVII, Number 2, pp. 52-54.

[8] Distributed by Folkways Records (Number FX 6007) 701 - 7th Avenue, New York, New York 10036.

CHAPTER SIX

CONCLUSION

Taken in its entirety, the proposed comprehensive musicianship curriculum may be too complex to be fully adopted by some band directors, particularly those working in small schools. When a director states that the teaching of comprehensive musicianship through band performance is a good idea, but that the approach is too complex and idealistic to be workable in his own program, one listens carefully. It could be argued that education is complex today, and that curriculum designs for other school subjects, such as mathematics, biology, and physics, are complex. It could also be argued that teaching is an idealistic art in that a teacher must constantly strive to achieve lofty goals and objectives. Doesn't he have to approach his students and subject matter with an idealistic attitude? Doesn't he have to maintain a positive attitude about what his students can achieve? Many times established goals and objectives are never fully achieved by all students due to practical and mitigating circumstances. But that is no matter to be unduly concerned about. The important thing is that the students continue to grow in their understanding, knowledge, and skill in the subject matter, and that they put forth their best efforts in accomplishing the tasks set before them.

Having said this, the problem still remains: How can the band director, particularly the one working in the small school, begin to implement the proposed curriculum within the confines of an existing program? This chapter addresses itself to the problem and presents specific suggestions for adapting the curriculum components in simplified form.

The Band Director in the Small School

The writer recognizes that there are directors working in small schools who do not have inordinate amounts of time to devote to band because they have to teach other music classes: music appreciation, chorus, general music, and so on. These are the same teachers who have the only band around that can march in the local Veterans Day parade and who are expected by the school board, parents, and sports fans to perform, perform, perform. In situations like these, the survival of the band program may depend on the director's willingness to march in parades and perform halftime shows at football games. If a director teaches in a school like this, then he should develop the marching band; first things first. In doing so, however, he must understand that the marching band is an entertainment medium and not an educational or aesthetic medium.[1] As such, it cannot be used effectively as a vehicle for teaching comprehensive musicianship. As an entertainment medium, the marching band cannot be considered a legitimate fine art subject in the school curriculum, lest the schools be in the business of entertainment instead of education. This is not to condemn the marching band or to suggest its elimination. The marching band definitely has a place in the school music program. In addition to supporting the athletic department and serving as the public relations arm of the school, the marching band can be used effectively to recruit new students and to build community support. The question is not whether the marching band should be eliminated from the music program, but rather, how much emphasis should be given to it. If the marching band is the primary performance medium, the band program is being justified on entertainment grounds. Hence, band will be considered an extracurricular activity. When school board members and those responsible for the fiscal management of a school system are faced with financial difficulties, extracurricular activities will be cut first; these are considered low priority items in most school budgets.[2] The implication is obvious: the survival of band as a *legitimate fine art subject in the school curriculum* is dependent upon the willingness of the band director to gradually shift emphasis, however slowly, toward a comprehensive musicianship curriculum based on aesthetic education. "The band director who can define the educational basis of his program in aesthetic terms will forge an argument which no administrator [parent or school board member] can break."[3]

Suggestions for Implementing the Curriculum in Simplified Form

It is not intended that the proposed curriculum be fully implemented in all band programs with equal application, or even that any single component, such as the unit study composition, be adopted in its fully developed form at first. The director should view the curriculum (components and strategies) as he would items on a menu. He may select the entire meal, appetizer, salad, main course, dessert, beverage, as one package; or, more often than not, he may order "a la carte," pick and choose those items that suit his taste. In either case, he should avoid a drastic change of diet.

The changeover from a traditional program to a comprehensive musicianship curriculum should be evolutionary rather than revolutionary. The director should proceed slowly at first and not try to accomplish too much at once. Because the idea of teaching comprehensive musicianship through band performance is relatively new,[4] many established directors may find the approach totally foreign to the "traditional way of doing things." Therefore, the director should implement the curriculum in stages by gradually adopting or expanding a single component each year. Not only do students need time to adjust to new modes of instruction, but the director may need time to experiment in order to find the best ways to adapt the curriculum to his own talents and teaching situation.

The proposed curriculum is unified, yet entirely flexible. It is unified in that there is one philosophical premise and one set of program objectives. It is flexible in that the instructional components and educational strategies can be readily adapted to fit the needs of individual band directors and their programs.

Unified: Context — Aesthetic Education
               Content — Blueprint of Objectives

Flexible: Curriculum Components — Unit Study Composition
                                         Special Study Unit
                                         Band Projects
                                         Source/Reference Notebook

Organizational and Teaching/Learning Strategies

Flexibility is the key word in adapting the curriculum. Each band director must evaluate the development stage of his program, the musical sophistication of his students (concepts and skills), and the time available for teaching band (performance commitments and course teaching load). He must then determine which of the curriculum components and strategies to adopt first, and in what form.

The following suggestions are offered to show how each component of the curriculum can be established initially in simplified form. Although the suggestions are directed specifically to the band director in the small school, they apply equally well to medium and large school band programs.

Band Projects: The most practical curriculum component to establish first is band projects. Even in small schools in which the only performing group is primarily a marching band, band projects can be implemented successfully. Band projects are enriching activities that provide students with additional learning opportunities and challenges to meet their varying needs and interests; they require little or no actual class teaching time, but do require a minimal amount of out-of-class work. To initiate the use of band projects in your program, follow these procedures: (1) Require your students to complete one of three types of band projects at least twice a year: a concert review, a research report, or a chamber music performance.[5] The triple-option plan is highly recommended at first. (2) Provide your students with an outline of the procedures and guidelines for completing each project. (3) Allow your students the option of devising their own projects with your approval (see Chapter Two, pp. 16-17). The last suggestion should be emphasized when introducing the assignment. Since there may be little time to initiate creative projects on a wide scale in the small school, it is especially important that students be encouraged to try their hand at arranging and composing as an optional band project. Even in relatively small, developing programs, there are at least two or three talented students who are capable of completing a creative project. If a student decides to arrange or compose a short composition, take time to rehearse and tape the piece so that the student can evaluate what he has done.

Source/Reference Notebook: If a traditional band handbook is currently in use, change the title and gradually expand it so that it will correlate with the establishment of other curriculum components. If a handbook is not in use, serious consideration should be given to writing one along lines suggested in Appendix A.[6] The materials to be included in the notebook may be very simple at first; for example, the guidelines for completing band projects, a short list of common musical terms, and the "Six Commandments for Developing Sight Reading Skill." As the curriculum evolves from one year to the next, the notebook will be augmented and expanded to include learning material developed in the process of teaching other instructional units. The advantages gained in using the source/reference notebook as a teaching/learning tool in the curriculum far outweigh the slight burden students will have to bear in carrying the notebooks to rehearsals along with their instruments and music folders.[7] When a student graduates or leaves the program, he will have accumulated a valuable compendium of music materials that can be referred to later on.

The Special Study Unit: Gradually incorporate one or two special study units into the curriculum each year. Special study units can be used to cover a wide range of band-related topics that will provide students with basic knowledge and skills. Most of these units should be taught in the training bands, beginning and intermediate levels. Highly developed learning guides need not be used. Instead, use simple instructional materials, such as study sheets, information outlines, worksheets, and so on. The following modifications are recommendations for each of the special study unit topics covered in Chapter Five.

Basic Conducting: Omit the learning guide. Teach basic conducting skill in the intermediate band when developing student responsiveness to the conductor's baton. Follow these procedures: daigram basic beat patterns on the chalkboard (a simple handout may also be used). Instruct the band to conduct the patterns as a group. Utilize at least two different beat styles, legato and staccato. Time permitting, cover one or more of the following conducting techniques: preparatory gestures, cutoffs, cueing, subdivided beats, dynamics, and other beat styles. Identify by observation individual students who catch on quickly and have graceful motions. Provide these students with an opportunity to conduct the band sometime during the year. If a student prepares a score and conducts in public, accept the performance in lieu of a band project.

Transposition and Scoring: Although this unit may have to be omitted in the small school in which time is a problem, each student should be taught the transposition of his or her own instrument, where sounding from the written page, as a basic objective. This knowledge is essential if the student is to understand the director's instructions during rehearsals. Of course, if a student decides to do an arrangement as a band project, the director may have to provide guidance somewhere along the way.

Acoustics, Tuning, and Intonation: Simplify this special study unit by covering only what is absolutely necessary to begin getting the students moving in the right direction. Although a learning guide need not be used for this unit, it is highly recommended that each student be provided with a tuning guide for his or her own instrument (see Chapter Five, Footnote 5). In addition, each student should be required to chart his or her own intonation with the stroboscope at least once a year.

Sight Reading: Teach this unit as suggested in Chapter Five; no change. Be sure that the music chosen for developing sight reading skill is relatively easy.

Fundamentals of Music: Correlate these mini-units with the development of instrumental skills in the training bands. Start with one or two units the first year; add new units gradually from one year to the next. The materials developed for these mini-units should be added to the source/reference notebook in the same way. Keep the materials as simple as possible at first to coincide with the conceptual understanding levels of the students. Zero in on upgrading aural skills, melodic, harmonic, and rhythmic, while working to improve instrumental skills.

Example: When training students to play major scales:

1. Teach the structure of the major scale:

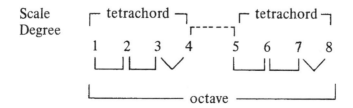

96

Whole Step (WS) = ⌊___⌋

Half Step (HS) = ∨

Two tetrachords connected by a whole step equal a major scale.

Tetrachord — a four-note group.

Octave — an eight-note group.

Scale — (Italian *scala* — ladder) a specific arrangement of pitches
(mostly whole and half steps) in ascending or descending
order. Scales provide composers with the tonal building
blocks for the construction of melodies and harmonies in
a composition.

2. Teach the basic rules for determining the key from the key signature:

Flat Keys — Count down four lines and spaces from the last
flat to the right or subtract one flat from the right.

Sharp Keys — Count up one line or space from the last sharp
to the right.

3. Teach aural discrimination of the intervals that occur between the first degree of the
scale and each of the other degrees of the scale. One good way to do this is to teach
students to play the following interval exercise:

Trumpet

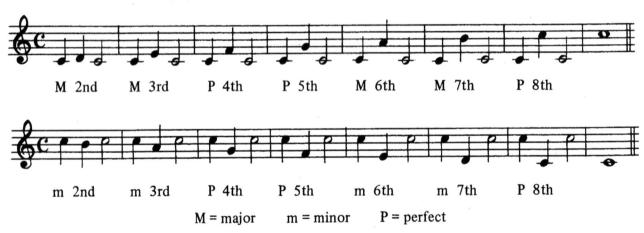

M = major   m = minor   P = perfect

When writing this exercise for students to practice and memorize (it should be applied to all
major scales), include the interval identifications as shown in the example.[8] Note that,
except for enharmonically spelled intervals, the only interval missing is the tritone (augmented
fourth or diminished fifth). Students who are taught to play and hear these basic intervals
will be better able to hear and understand the tonal structure of the music they are playing.

The information given on the opposite page is typical of the type of learning material that could be used when teaching a mini-study unit on the fundamentals of music. The material could be designed into a student practice-study sheet or included in the source/reference notebook. Similar concept-skill teaching materials could also be developed for use when teaching students to play articulations, dynamics, rhythms and meters, chords, other scale forms, and so on. It doesn't take any longer to teach this way because students are building a conceptual understanding of what they are playing—knowledge that is transferable and therefore time-saving in the long run.

Common Musical Terms: Compile a basic list of musical terms that is appropriate for your program and include the list with brief definitions in the source/reference notebook.[9] New students entering the program should be required to study the terms and a brief written quiz should be given to insure that they complete the assignment.

Instrument Care and Maintenance: Teach this unit as outlined in Chapter Five; no change.

The Unit Study Composition: Before discussing how the unit study composition can be utilized in simplified form, it is necessary to clarify one important point concerning the guide for score analysis given in Chapter Three (see under "Analysis—Music Structure," pp. 32 ff). The reasons for presenting the guide in a detailed form are twofold: (1) to show how a score can be analyzed systematically, and (2) to present a comprehensive list of subconcepts that can be found in a wide body of band literature. Undoubtedly, the guide is too comprehensive to be followed in its entirety by the band director. The same may be said for the model unit study composition given in Chapter Four. The lesson plan for *Spectrum* presents more material than is likely to be used by most band directors. As a model, however, it shows what can be done in very creative and highly innovative programs. *Spectrum* was chosen for the model because it offered many possibilities for teaching comprehensive musicianship. Most works for band are not as rich in teaching/learning possibilities. The complexity of the model should not deter the director from considering the approach. It is stated at the end of Chapter Three that the lesson plan format can be "simplified," "modified," or "adapted"; and that all seven concept areas need not be covered for each unit study composition selected. Indeed, the director working in the small school may wish to select only one or two concept areas for emphasis, and he may want to utilize simpler modes of instruction.[10]

The following simplified instructional modes may be used in lieu of the more complex teaching procedures utilized in the model unit study composition. Directors who wish to begin rather conservatively at first should start with mode one. Each instructional mode is slightly more involved than the one that precedes it.

Instructional Mode 1 The director relates basic information about the unit study composition during breaks that naturally occur in the rehearsal. In this procedure, analytical, stylistic, and historical information is intermittently interjected to help students better understand and interpret the work they are playing. To be sure that the information will be used in future music making, the presentation should be based on a predetermined framework of concepts and objectives (see Chapter One for ideas). Failure to do so will result in an instructional process that lacks continuity. There are two disadvantages to using this instructional mode: (1) the educational process is still teacher-centered, and (2) there is no concrete means for evaluating student learning, except of course, a more enlightened performance.

Instructional Mode 2 The director develops and distributes a simplified study guide or other appropriate material related to the work under study. The material should be geared to the understanding levels of the students and should focus on developing concepts and skills related to the structure and style of the music. A simplified flow chart analysis, such as the one given on page 37, may be all that is needed to reveal both the internal and external structure of the unit study composition.[11] Since the students will be assigned to study the material outside of class, this instructional mode is relatively easy to administer. To be sure that students understand what is given to them, however, the material should be covered in class. In addition, some form of evaluation should be used to ascertain the degree of learning that takes place.

Instructional Mode 3 The band director instructs his students to complete an out of class listening and reading assignment related to the work currently being rehearsed. This procedure is thoroughly covered as a separate teaching/learning strategy in Chapter Two (see p. 15). All that need be added here is that the assignment should be made optional at first. With a quick show of hands during a rehearsal, the director can determine how many students have completed the assignment. Eventually the assignment should be required of all students. When this occurs, take time during one rehearsal period to evaluate the student's work. The evaluation can be in the form of a brief oral, written, or listening quiz.

In gradually adopting the unit study composition as the primary instructional component in the curriculum, it may be necessary to curtail the yearly number of band performances. No one who is unfamiliar with a given program can suggest what would be a reasonable number of performances; there are too many variables from one program to another. All that can be said is that the director who is under constant pressure to perform will only have time to drill students in preparation for the next performance. In situations like this, the performance schedule dictates what transpires in the rehearsal hall. As Joseph Labuta aptly comments:

> This is certainly a confusion of means and ends. If the band rehearsal is really a place to study music, concerts should be a logical outgrowth of learning activities. Public performance, then, is a summary of the learning that has taken place in the rehearsal classes, where the important activities have occurred. Performance is primarily a means, not an end.[12]

Each band director must resolve in his own mind the basic philosophical question concerning the role of the performing ensemble in the school curriculum. Is the purpose of the school band solely "performance," or is it "education through performance"? In other words, is performance the ultimate goal of the curriculum, or is performance primarily a means for achieving more lasting objectives.

It must be clearly understood that the proposed curriculum is not antiperformance. The band must continue to work toward achieving the highest level of performance it is capable of attaining. Performance standards must not be slighted in any way. Indeed, a high level of performance is a necessary condition for any comprehensive musicianship curriculum of this type. Furthermore, evidence has shown that when students are taught both concepts and skills through the performance repertoire, they perform as well or better because they understand the music they are playing.

The Student Liaison and Planning Committee

One of the best ways to successfully implement the proposed curriculum is to organize a liaison and planning committee within the band and to involve students in the process of adopting new teaching/learning ideas. In general, student learning activities should arise out of decisions and choices of the learners. Organizing a student liaison and planning committee will provide both the director and students with a forum for a healthy communication of ideas. The director can present his goals and objectives, explain what he is trying to accomplish educationally and musically, and inform students about what is expected of them. Students may not automatically understand or agree with the director's viewpoint, unless he informs them of his philosophy, goals, and objectives. In turn, student representatives who serve on the committee can provide the director with valuable input concerning the band's attitude and responses to newly-planned activities. Student responses to even the simplest modes of instruction may not be encouraging at first. Bandsmen who have not been exposed to comprehensive musicianship training in the past may resist the approach initially. A typical student comment is: "Band was never like this before." Consequently, it may take time to convince students of the validity of the approach. General acceptance of the curriculum by students largely depends on the attitude, commitment, and enthusiasm of the band director. He must not only be excited about the curriculum and convinced of what it can accomplish, but he must convey this enthusiasm and conviction to his students.

Guidelines for Organizing a Student Liaison and Planning Committee

One student representative from each section of the band is elected by the members of the section to serve on the committee. Although section leaders may serve if elected, they should not be appointed automatically. Experience has shown that the best procedure for selecting committee members is for each section to elect their representative by majority vote. Just prior to the election, the director should explain the purposes of the committee and outline the responsibilities that will be entrusted to those who are elected.

Section	Number of Representatives
Flutes	1
Double Reeds	1
Clarinets	1
Saxophones	1
French Horns	1
Trumpets/Cornets	1
Trombones	1
Baritone Horns/Tubas	1
Percussion	1
One additional "at large" member may be appointed by the director if desired.	1
Total Number	10

Within the committee of ten members, an executive subcommittee of four may be elected: woodwind, brass, percussion, and one "at large" member. The executive subcommittee can serve as the band officers if desired: President, Vice President, Secretary, Treasurer.

The liaison and planning committee need not be confined solely to matters pertaining to the curriculum. The committee can work on any matter relevant to their participation in band: selection of the repertoire,[13] planning of performance commitments, rules and regulations, dress, rehearsal and concert protocol, auditioning requirements, challenging procedures, fund raising, and so on.

If the student liaison and planning committee is established along democratic lines such as those outlined above, it can become an excellent vehicle for developing the leadership abilities of individual bandsmen. In addition, each student in the band will begin to feel that he is playing an important role in the process of his own education.

To summarize, the major goal of a comprehensive musicianship curriculum is to develop a musical person: one who has an in-depth understanding of basic musical concepts related to the structural and stylistic elements of music, a general knowledge of music as a creative art form of man in a historical context, and the skills to perform musical operations: play an instrument, read notation, demonstrate aural imagery, use notation as a means of communication. The band director who adopts the proposed curriculum and focuses his instruction on achieving these attainable goals will cultivate in his students lasting musical habits, attitudes, and appreciations that will remain with them after they leave the program, and will continue to provide them with a source of pleasure and enrichment throughout their lives.

Footnotes (Chapter Six)

[1] For a clarification of the question: Is the marching band an aesthetic medium or an entertainment medium?, see David Whitwell, *A New History of Wind Music* (Evanston, Illinois: The Instrumentalist Company, 1972), Chapter VII "Toward a New Philosophy," pp. 74-77.

[2] In recent years, the *Music Educators Journal* has given many accounts of such cuts and the need to justify the music curriculum on aesthetic grounds.

[3] Whitwell, *op. cit.*, p. 74.

[4] The writer has observed a few outstanding directors who have been teaching comprehensive musicianship through their performing ensembles for years without calling it that. In fact, many of the strategies for teaching comprehensive musicianship suggested in Chapter Two were gleaned from practicing band directors working in both large and small schools. The strategies are not new. What is new, however, is the integration of these strategies into a unified, yet flexible, curriculum model that has content, continuity, and evaluation.

[5] A solo or small ensemble performance at a city, county, or state music festival should be accepted as a band project.

[6] Most of the source/reference material listed in Part II-B of Appendix A is published in *Rehearsal Handbook for Band and Orchestra Students* by Robert Garofalo (Meredith Music Publications, 170 N.E. 33rd St., Ft. Lauderdale, Florida 33307).

[7] For years, this writer was frustrated in teaching band because he lacked an effective way to codify learning materials used in the instructional process. With the development of the source/reference notebook, however, the problem was resolved.

[8] When writing technical exercises for the full band to play, only five separate parts need to be completed: (1) a treble clef part for nontransposing instruments: piccolo, flute, oboe, and mallet keyboard; (2) a bass clef part for nontransposing instruments: trombone, baritone horn, bassoon, tuba, and string bass; (3) a treble clef part for $B^\flat$ transposing instruments: cornet/trumpet, $B^\flat$ soprano, bass, and contrabass clarinets, $B^\flat$ tenor saxophone, and baritone horn (treble clef); (4) a treble clef part for F transposing instruments: French horn and English horn; and (5) a treble clef part for $E^\flat$ alto and baritone saxophones, $E^\flat$ soprano, alto and contra-alto carinets. Exercises should be written in two or three octaves to coincide with the normal playing ranges of the instruments.

[9] A good working vocabulary of terms with definitions is published in *Rehearsal Handbook for Band and Orchestra Students* (see footnote 6).

[10] In programs where the major performing ensemble is primarily a marching band, at least one indoor concert is given during the year, usually at Christmastime or in the spring. In programs like this, the director can begin to teach comprehensive musicianship via the unit study composition in simplified form by selecting one work from the projected program for study.

[11] The material may focus on only one core concept and one or more subconcepts. Example: *First Suite in E Flat* by Gustav Holst – CONCEPT: Melody, SUBCONCEPT: Thematic Transformation. On a student study sheet, show how the opening chaconne theme is transformed and utilized throughout all three movements of this tightly knit composition. For an excellent analysis of the work, see Charles Gallagher, "Thematic Derivations in the Holst First Suite in E Flat," *Journal of Band Research* (Winter 1965) Volume I, Number 2, pp. 6-10.

[12]Joseph Labuta, "The Band as a Learning Laboratory," *Music Educators Journal* (January 1976) Volume 62, Number 5, p. 49.

[13]To involve students in the process of selecting the performance repertoire and to determine their likes and dislikes concerning the same, follow these procedures: draw up a handout sheet listing the works sight-read during the special study unit on sight reading. Distribute the sheet at the conclusion of the unit, and ask the students to indicate which works they like or dislike; written comments indicating why they like or dislike a particular work should be encouraged. Instruct the liaison and planning committee to collect the forms and study them. Call a meeting of the committee and discuss each work. Committee members are to reflect the general opinions of the members of their sections gleaned from the information given in the handout sheet. Take note of strong preferences either for or against each composition. Evaluate the input and decide on the repertoire the band will play. If the repertoire coincides with the musical preferences of the band members, you will have no trouble getting them to practice their parts. If it does not, you should explain why you have chosen the music. The procedures outlined here are highly recommended because they compel students to utilize their judicial faculties by directing them to make value judgments about the music they are playing. Furthermore, the discussion carried on in the committee meetings can be enlightening for band directors and students alike.

APPENDIX A

SUGGESTED CONTENT OUTLINE FOR THE SOURCE/REFERENCE NOTEBOOK

Part I of the outline that follows includes general information typically found in school band hand-books. Part II includes an overview of the curriculum and basic source/reference material that will be used regularly in teaching comprehensive musicianship. Publishing an outline of the new curriculum in the notebook will enable both students and parents to know the content and organization of the band program. The information can also be used to inform administrators, counselors, music supervisors, and other interested individuals about the curriculum.

Procedure: Upon entering the band program for the first time, the young instrumentalist is given a copy of the source/reference notebook. He keeps the notebook until he graduates from the school. The notebook is evaluated periodically and turned in to the director at the end of each school year. If the student wishes to retain his notebook over the summer, he may do so only with special permission from the director. Graduating seniors and students who are permanently leaving the program are allowed to take their notebooks with them. The notebook should be a loose-leaf, open-ended type in which the student can add all distributed and accumulated materials acquired during his tenure in the program.

Since the writing and reproduction of the notebook will be both time-consuming and costly, each band member and his parents should be required to read and sign an agreement form stating the student's responsibilities for taking care of it.

Source/Reference Notebook

Content Outline

Parent and Student Agreement Form

Part I General Information Handbook

Introduction (Words of Welcome)

Brief History of the Program

Course Offerings and Descriptions:
      Performing Ensembles
      Schedule
      Credit
      Auditions
      Section Seating (challenges)

Section Leaders' Responsibilities
Officers and Responsibilities

Organizational Guidelines (Policies and Procedures):

Rehearsal and Concert Protocol
School-Owned Instruments and Equipment (rental contracts, band uniforms, and so on)
Music and Music Folders
Private Lessons
Purchase of Quality Instruments

Additional:

Parent Booster Association (fund raising activities)
Music Awards and Scholarships
Music Clubs or Societies

Part II Curriculum Overview and Source/Reference Materials

A. Curriculum Overview

Statement of Philosophy

Blueprint of Objectives

Curriculum Components:

Instructional Units
    Unit Study Compositions
    Special Study Units
Band Projects
Source/Reference Notebook

Grading Policies and Procedures: Include comments on newly-established modes of assessment based on stated behavioral objectives.

Student Liaison and Planning Committee

B. Source/Reference Material

Band Projects: Include a comprehensive list of acceptable band projects and format outlines for projects, such as research reports, book reports, article resumes, concert critiques, record reviews, and so on.

Fundamentals of Music

1. Keyboard, Great Staff, and Clefs
2. Scale Types and Patterns
3. Intervals
4. Key Cycle and Key Signatures
5. Chord Types
6. Reference Chart of Common Chords
7. Meters
8. Note Values and Rests
9. Reference Chart of Common Rhythms

Glossary of Common Musical Terms and Symbols
1. Dynamic Markings
2. Tempo Markings
3. Stylistic Terms
4. Miscellaneous

Six Commandments for Developing Sight Reading Skill

Transposition Reference Chart

Brass Instrument Relationships Chart

Woodwind Instrument Relationships Chart

Historical Style Periods of Western Art Music

Contemporary (c. 1900 to Present)
Romantic (c. 1825 to 1900)
Classical (c. 1750 to 1825)
Baroque (c. 1600 to 1750)
Renaissance (c. 1450 to 1600)
Late Middle Ages (c. 1000 to 1450)

APPENDIX B
SELECTED BIBLIOGRAPHY AND
DISCOGRAPHY WITH ANNOTATIONS

Part I   Comprehensive Musicianship Source Materials

The band director having committed himself to exploring the possibilities of teaching comprehensive musicianship through his performance organization(s) will need to find additional materials to reinforce and expand his own attitudes and competencies. The following list of publications is offered to further assist the ensemble director in developing a comprehensive musicianship program. All quoted annotations were taken from the sources themselves or from advertisements.

Band Music Notes (revised edition 1979) by Norman Smith and Albert Stoutamire. Neil A. Kjos Music Company, 4382 Jutland Drive, San Diego, California 92117.   Composer information and program notes for over 600 band favorites.

Basic Band Repertory (1980) by Frederick Fennell. The Instrumentalist Company, 1418 Lake Street, Evanston, Illinois 60204. British band classics—from the conductor's point of view.

Comprehensive Musicianship: An Anthology of Evolving Thought (1971).
Contemporary Music Project (CMP$_5$). Music Educators National Conference, 1902 Association Drive, Reston, Virginia 22091. "A discussion of the first ten years (1959-1969) of the Contemporary Music Project, particularly as they relate to the development of the theory of comprehensive musicianship, as reported in articles and speeches by those closely associated with the Project."

Comprehensive Musicianship Through Band Performance (several volumes for high school and junior high school band, 1972-1973) by Brent Heisinger. Addison-Wesley Publishing Company, Sand Hill Road, Menlo Park, California 94025. Each book contains several complete teaching units "each having its core for study a composition for full band. The units comprise lessons that are considered to be models for the study of musical concepts. Each lesson includes student objectives stated in behavioral terms, definitions of terms related to the concepts under study, and activities for developing comprehensive musicianship and evaluating lesson objectives. Activities for full band and chamber composition ensembles are provided and correlated." The materials were developed by the Research and Development Group of the University of Hawaii for the Hawaii Music Curriculum Project. Teacher and student editions available.

Creative Musicianship Band Series (1981) by Robert Garofalo and Garwood Whaley. The Heritage Music Press, 501 E. Third St., P. O. Box 802, Dayton, Ohio 45401. Imaginative arrangements for young musicians with optional activities for stimulating creativity.

Essentials of Musicianship for the Band (1970) by Maurice C. Whitney. Warner Brothers Music, 75 Rockefeller Plaza, New York, New York 10019. "A textbook for musical understanding with practical examples to play in the band rehearsal." Ten study units covering the Tools of Music, Tone Production, Rhythm, Melody, Harmony, Counterpoint, Form, Musical Terms, Style, and Music History. Each instrument book is divided into two parts: a study text and musical examples.

Four Centuries for Band by Philip Gordon (editor). Carl Fischer, Inc., 56-62 Cooper Square, New York, New York 10003. "An excellent collection of music of the past four centuries for teaching and concert use, arranged and edited with complete program notes." Also available for brass ensemble—*Four Centuries for Brass.*

Heritage Americana (1982) by Robert Garofalo and Mark Elrod (editors). Neil A. Kjos Music Company, 4382 Jutland Drive, San Diego, California 92117. A unique collection of Civil War military brass band music edited for modern brass ensemble with historical annotations.

Insights Into Music Series by Maurice C. Whitney (editor). Alfred Music Company 15335 Morrison Street, P. O. Box 5964, Sherman Oaks, California 91413. "A curriculum for concert band that combines understanding with performance. Turns each band rehearsal into an enjoyable educational learning experience." Several full band arrangements of works from four historical periods: Renaissance, baroque, classical, and romantic. Each selection includes notes about the performance practices and compositional techniques of the historical style period.

Music in General Education (1965) by Karl D. Ernst and Charles L. Gary (editors). Music Educator National Conference, Reston, Virginia. Includes descriptions of many activities that can broaden the musical experiences of students in instrumental performing ensembles. The activities and experiences are organized according to specific content areas: Elements of Music, Form and Design in Music, and Interpretive Aspects of Music. Contains source lists of performance music, films, filmstrips, recordings, and books that relate to each content area.

Performing Music With Understanding (2 volumes—1970, 1971) by Charles R. Hoffer and Donald K. Anderson. Wadsworth Publishing Company, Inc., Belmont, California 94002. A largely self-instructional programmed style designed to support regular rehearsal and performance activities in high school bands, orchestras and choral groups. Offers many suggestions for student projects in research and analysis. Includes lists of appropriate music and books. Teacher and student editions available.

Rehearsal Handbook for Band and Orchestra Students (1983) by Robert Garofalo. Meredith Music Publications, 170 N. E. 33rd St., Ft. Lauderdale, Florida 33307. Includes rehearsal enrichment study units covering the fundamentals of music, acoustics, tuning and intonation, music terms and symbols, sight reading, conducting and music history.

The Sounds of Contemporary Harmonies: Made Easy for Bands at All Levels (1971) by Lawrence Weiner and Howard Lerner. Southern Music Company, Inc., 110 Broadway, San Antonio, Texas 78206. "A unique aid to the performance of modern compositions; scales, harmonized as chorales, using twelve contemporary harmonic devices; playable at all teaching levels, since rhythmic and technical problems are eliminated; playable by any size group." Educational objectives for each lesson and a glossary of musical terms are included.

Teaching Musicianship in the High School Band (1972) by Joseph A. Labuta. Parker Publishing Company, West Nyack, New York 10994. Organized as a curriculum outline or guide that begins with the structural elements of music and progresses through musical form to a chronological presentation of historical styles. Consistently emphasizes the relationship of structure and style to performance.

Part II   Sources for Performance Literature

The following list of sources has been compiled for your immediate convenience. The list includes sources for solo, chamber, and large ensemble music. Standard publishers' catalogues have not been included, but of course, these should be consulted. Other selective and recommended lists of performance literature may be available through your local and state music educators associations.

Band Music Guide (eighth edition, 1982), The Instrumentalist Company, 1418 Lake Street, Evanston, Illinois 60204. A comprehensive listing of published band compositions, band collections, solos and ensembles with band, band methods, marching band maneuvers, and fanfares.

Brass Ensemble Music Guide (1978) compiled by Paul G. Anderson. The Instrumentalist Company, 1418 Lake Street, Evanston, Illinois 60204. A comprehensive listing of compositions published for brass ensembles (from two to ten or more instruments). Includes a composer index and key to publishers.

Brass Players' Guide (1982-83) compiled by Robert King. Robert King Music Company, 112 A Main St., North Easton, Massachusets, 02356. A comprehensive guide to brass music of all publishers.

An Evaluation of Compositions for Wind Band According to Specific Criteria of Serious Artistic Merit (1978) by Acton E. Ostling, Jr., University Microfilms International, 300 North Zeeb Road, Ann Arbor, Michigan 48106. Includes several cross indexed lists of wind band music judged to be of high artistic merit by an outstanding panel of conductors.

Original Manuscript Music for Wind and Percussion Instruments (1973) compiled by Richard K. Weerts. Music Educators National Conference, Reston, Virginia. Over 400 listings of music available only in manuscript form with instrumentation, difficulty, and composer's address. Updated from the 1964 edition.

Selective Music Lists—Instrumental Solos and Ensembles (1979) compiled cooperatively by MENC and associated organizations. Music Educators National Conference, Reston, Virginia. Qualitative listings of performance literature.

Solo and Ensemble Literature for Percussion (1978) compiled by F. Michael Combs. Percussive Arts Society, 214 West Main Street, P. O. Box 697, Urbana, Illinois 61801-0697. A comprehensive listing of graded percussion music organized by instrumentation. Includes percussion solos with band.

Wind Ensemble Literature (Second edition, revised 1975) compiled by Robert Reynolds, et. al. University of Wisconsin Bands, 455 North Park Street, Madison, Wisconsin 53706. An excellent catalogue of over 4,000 selected compositions for wind ensemble, wind ensemble with instrumental or vocal soloists, and wind ensemble and chorus. Includes composer, title, specific instrumentation, publisher, and recordings for each entry.

Woodwind Music Guide (1982) compiled by Himie Voxman and Lyle Merriman. The Instrumentalist Company, 1418 Lake Street, Evanston, Illinois 60204. A comprehensive listing of compositions published for one or more woodwind instruments. Each listing includes title, composer, arranger, editor, publisher, and instrumentation. Compositions are grouped according to the number of instruments represented, and within each category, by different types of instrumental combinations.

Part III   Sources for Band Recordings

For recordings of the Eastman Wind Ensemble under Frederick Fennell and Donald Hunsberger, consult standard record catalogues such as the Schwann Catalogue. Fennell's classic recordings (Mercury Records) made in the 1950s and 1960s are periodically reissued under the Philips label. For superb recordings of outstanding literature for various wind ensembles performed by the Netherlands Wind Ensemble (Philips) and the Cleveland Symphonic Winds (Telarc Records), consult standard record catalogues.

Cornell University Wind Ensemble Records. For a list of recordings available, write to Maurice Stith, Band Office, Lincoln Hall, Cornell University, Ithaca, New York 14850.

Crest Records. Crest Records is the authorized recording company for many national music conventions: College Band Directors National Association, Music Educators National Conference, Midwest Band and Orchestra Clinic. Recordings are available of selected convention performances by outstanding bands and wind ensembles. For catalogues, write to Golden Crest Records, Inc., 220 Broadway, Huntington Station, New York 11746.

Educational Record Reference Library. Belwin-Mills Publishing Corporation, 25 Deshon Drive, Melville, New York 11746. A comprehensive series of band recordings by college, high school, and professional groups. Over thirty-six twelve-inch LP albums have been issued. Although the Educational Record Reference Library is no longer published, it remains a major source for recordings of band music.

University of Illinois Concert Band Recordings. Excellent recorded performances of classic band literature conducted by Mark Hindsley and his successor Harry Begian. The complete band works of Percy Grainger are available in a two-record set. For a catalogue, write to the University of Illinois Bands, 1103 South Sixth Street, Champaign, Illinois 61820.

APPENDIX C
SELECTED REPERTOIRE

The following lists of music are classified according to historical periods of Western art music. Part I includes a selected and graded list of music for concert band. Only original band music by master composers is listed under Twentieth Century, Romantic, and Classical periods. Many of these works are established "band classics." The works listed under Renaissance-Baroque are illustrative of the many excellent band transcriptions and arrangements of music from early historical periods. Part II includes a selected and graded list of original chamber music for wind sextets, septets, octets, nonets, and large chamber wind and percussion ensembles. Standard wind quintet, quartet, and trio literature has not been included because this music is generally known and readily available.

The asterisk (*) found in the left-hand column indicates that the composers have written additional music for concert band or chamber wind ensembles.

Grading System: M = Medium

MD = Moderately Difficult

D = Difficult

Generally, this system parallels the standard festival grading system developed by the National Interscholastic Music Activities Commission of the Music Educators National Conference.

For names and addresses of the publishers indicated by the initial code, see Key to Publishers, page 120. Four of the publishers listed are singled out here for special comment.

CFP   C. F. Peters Corporation publishes the American Wind Symphony Editions, Robert Austin Boudreau, editor. Includes many excellent works by eminent composers commissioned by the American Wind Symphony Orchestra.

MCA   Music Corporation of America publishes the MCA Symphonic Wind Ensemble Editions, Donald Hunsberger, editor. Each work in this series contains elements of the basic principles of the symphonic wind ensemble concept—specified instrumentation, single performer approach, and development of individual tone colors. The instrumentation ranges from the components of the orchestral wind section to the full complement of the symphonic wind ensemble as illustrated by the Eastman Wind Ensemble and its companion organizations.

MR   Musica Rara publishes several editions of early wind music: Venetian Brass Music of the Early Sixteenth and Seventeenth Centuries; Moravian Brass Music; Tower Brass Music of Johann Pezel and Anton Reiche; and, early music for crumhorns, cornettos, recorders, trombones, and so on.

WIND   Wind Instrument's New Dawn Society is a performance source library specializing in early, mostly original, music for band and chamber wind ensembles.

Part I   Concert Band Literature

Composer-Arranger	Title	Grade	Publisher
	Twentieth Century		
* Badings, Henk	*Concerto for Flute and Wind Orchestra*	D	CFP
Barber, Samuel	*Commando March*	MD	GS
Bassett, Leslie	*Designs, Images and Textures*	D	CFP
* Bennett, Robert Russell	*Suite of Old American Dances*	MD	CHAP
* Benson, Warren	*The Leaves are Falling*	D	EBM
	The Solitary Dancer	M	MCA
* Copland, Aaron	*An Outdoor Overture*	MD	B&H
	Emblems	D	B&H
	Lincoln Portrait (with narrator)	MD	B&H
* Cowell, Henry	*Celtic Set*	M	GS
	Hymn and Fuguing Tune No. 1	M	MCA
* Creston, Paul	*Celebration Overture*, Op. 61	D	SHAW
	Concerto for Alto Saxophone and Band	D	GS (Rental)
	Concerto for Marimba and Band	MD	AMP
* Dahl, Ingolf	*Sinfonietta for Band*	MD	AB
* Dello Joio, Norman	*Fantasies on a Theme by Haydn*	M	EBM
	Songs of Abelard (optional solo voice)	MD	EBM
	Variants on a Medieval Tune	MD	EBM
Elgar, Edward	*The Severn Suite* (originally for brass band)	MD	SF
* Giannini, Vittorio	*Praeludium and Allegro*	D	COL
	Variations and Fugue	D	COL

Composer-Arranger	Title	Grade	Publisher
* Grainger, Percy	*Colonial Song*	M	CFP
	Children's March (Over the Hills and Far Away)	M	GS
	Irish Tune from County Derry	M	GS
	Lincolnshire Posy	D	CFP
	Shepherd's Hey	MD	CFP
* Hanson, Howard	*Chorale and Alleluia*	MD	CFP
* Hindemith, Paul	*Konzertmusik für Blasorchester*, Op. 41	D	BM (Rental)
	Symphony in B♭	D	AMP
* Holst, Gustav	*First Suite in E♭*	M	B&H
	Hammersmith: Prelude and Scherzo	D	B&H
	Second Suite in F	MD	B&H
* Hovhaness, Alan	*Symphony No. 4*, Op. 165	MD	CFP
* Husa, Karel	*Music for Prague*	D	AMP
* Ives, Charles	*Country Band March*	MD	TP
Mennin, Peter	*Canzona*	MD	CFP
* Milhaud, Darius	*Suite Francaise*	MD	LEE
* Nelhybel, Vaclav	*Two Symphonic Movements*	M	COL
* Persichetti, Vincent	*Chorale Prelude: Turn Not Thy Face*	M	EV
	Divertimento	MD	TP
	Masquerade for Band, Op. 102	MD	EV
	Psalm	MD	EV
	Symphony No. 6, Op. 69	D	EV
Piston, Walter	*Thunbridge Fair*	MD	B&H
Rogers, Bernard	*Three Japanese Dances*	D	TP
Schoenberg, Arnold	*Theme and Variations*, Op. 43a	D	GS
* Schuller, Gunther	*Meditations*	MD	AMP
* Schuman, William	*Chester Overture*	MD	TP
	George Washington Bridge	MD	GS
	When Jesus Wept	MD	MM
* Shostakovich, Dimitri	*Festive Overture*, Op. 96	D	MCA
Stravinsky, Igor	*Circus Polka*	D	AMP

Composer-Arranger	Title	Grade	Publisher
Vaughan Williams, Ralph	*English Folksong Suite*	M	B&H
	Flourish for Wind Band	M	OX
	Toccata Marziale	MD	B&H
	Sea Songs	M	B&H
Walton, William	*Crown Imperial: A Coronation March*	D	B&H

Romantic

Nineteenth-century original band music edited for modern instrumentation.

Composer-Arranger	Title	Grade	Publisher
Berlioz, Hector	*Symphonie Funèbre et Triomphale* (Symphony for Band), Op. 15	MD	WIND
* Donizetti, Gaetano	*March for the Sultan Abdul Medjid*	MD	MER
Mendelssohn-Bartholdy, Felix	*Overture for Winds,* Op. 24 (based on 1826 autograph score)	MD	LM
* Rossini, Gioacchino	*March for the Sultan Abdul Medjid*	MD	MER
	Three Marches for the Marriage of the Duke of Orleans	MD	GS
	Scherzo for Band	MD	PM
Wagner, Richard	*Huldigungsmarsch* (Homage March)	MD	SHAW
	Trauersinfonie (Funeral Symphony)	M	AMP

Classical

Late eighteenth-century original band music edited for modern instrumentation.

Composer-Arranger	Title	Grade	Publisher
Catel, Simone	*Overture in C*	MD	MER
	Symphonie Militaire	M	BOO
Gossec, Francois Joseph	*Classic Overture in C*	MD	MER
	Military Symphony in F	M	MER
	Suite for Band	M	COL
Hummel, Joseph	*Three Marches for Band*	M	GS
Jadin, Hyacinthe	*Overture in F* (1795)	M	COL
Jadin, Louis	*Symphonie for Band*	M	SHAW
Mehúl, Étienne-Henri	*Overture in F*	M	SM
Paer, Ferdinando	*Two Napoleonic Marches*	M	GM

Composer-Arranger	Title	Grade	Publisher

Baroque-Renaissance

Composer-Arranger	Title	Grade	Publisher
Bach-Chidester	*Passacaglia in C Minor*	MD	BM
Bach-Goldman & Leist	*Fantasia in G Major*	MD	MER
Bach-Holst	*Fugue à la Gigue*	MD	B&H
Bach-Hunsberger	*Passacaglia and Fugue in C Minor*	MD	GS
Bach-Moehlman	*Preludes and Fugues* (in B♭, F, G, and D Minor)	M	FITZ
Byrd-Jacob	*William Byrd Suite*	MD	B&H
Frescobaldi-Slocum	*Toccata*	M	MILL
Frescobaldi-Brunelli	*Praeludium and Fugue*	M	CHAP
Gabrieli, A.-Gardner	*Chorale St. Marks*	M	STAFF
Gabrieli, G.-Schaefer	*Sonata Pian e Forte*	M	EV
Handel-Kay	*Water Music*	M	TP
Handel-Schaefer	*Royal Fireworks Music*	MD	HM
Purcell-Gardner	*Fanfare and Rondo*	M	STAFF
Vivaldi-Cacavas	*Concerto Grosso in D Minor*	M	CHAP

Part II   Chamber Wind Ensemble Literature

Original sextet, septet, octet, nonet, and large chamber wind ensemble music.

Twentieth Century

Composer-Arranger	Title	Grade	Publisher
Adler, Samuel	*Music for Eleven* (Suite for Woodwinds & Percussion) 2 fl (pic), ob, cl, bass cl, bsn, timp, 4 perc	M	OX
Copland, Aaron	*Fanfare for the Common Man* 3 trp, 4 hrn, 3 tbn, tub, timp, 2 perc	D	B&H
Dukas, Paul	*Fanfare for La Peri* 3 trp, 4 hrn, 3 tbn, tub	MD	ED

Composer	Title	Grade	Publisher
* Grainger, Percy A.	*Hill Song No. 2* pic, 3 fl, 3 ob (erd ob opt), E hrn, 2 bsn, cbsn (st bass), E♭ cl, 3 B♭ cl, alto cl, bass cl, 4 sax, 2 trp, 2 hrn, cym	MD	LEE
* Hartley, Walter	*Concerto for Twenty-Three Wind Instruments* pic, 2 fl, 2 ob, E hrn, 2 cl, bass cl, 2 bsn, cbsn, 4 hrn, 3 trp, 3 tbn, tub	MD	RM
* Hindemith, Paul	*Geschwindmarsch* (from Symphony Serena) pic, 2 fl, 2 ob, E hrn, 2 cl, bass cl, 2 bsn, cbsn, 4 hrn, 2 trp, 2 tbn, tub, celesta, timp, 2 perc	D	EA
	Septett für Blasinstrumente (1948) fl, ob, cl, trp, hrn, bass cl, bsn	D	PIC
Jacob, Gordon	*Old Wine in New Bottles* 2 fl (pic), 2 ob, 2 cl, 2 bsn, cbsn (opt), 2 hrn, 2 trp (opt)	M	OX
Krenek, Ernst	*Three Merry Marches, Op. 44* fl, ob, E♭ cl, 3 B♭ cl, 2 trp, 2 hrn, tbn, tub, timp, 2 perc	M	BOO
Kurka, Robert	*The Good Soldier Schweik Suite, Op. 22* pic, fl, ob, E hrn, cl, bass cl, bsn cbsn, 3 hrn, 2 trp, tbn, timp, perc	MD	WEIN
* Milhaud, Darius	*Symphony No. 5* pic, fl, ob, E hrn, bass cl, 2 bsn, 2 hrn	MD	TP (Rental)
* Nelhybel, Vaclav	*Ancient Hungarian Dances* 3 trp, hrn, 3 tbn, bar, tub 3-6 perc (opt)	MD	COL
Persichetti, Vincent	*Serenade No. 1 for Ten Wind Instruments* fl, ob, cl, 2 hrn, bsn, 2 trp, tbn, tub	MD	EV
Poulenc, Francis	*Suite Francaise* (d'après Claude Gervaise XVIe siècle) 2 ob, 2 bsn, 2 trp, 3 tbn, piano, 2 perc	MD	TP (Rental)

116

Composer	Title	Grade	Publisher
Read, Gardner	*Nine by Six* (Suite for Wind Instruments) fl (pic), ob (E hrn), cl (bass cl), hrn, trp, bsn	MD	CFP
Reed, Alfred	*Double Wind Quintet* fl, ob, cl, bsn, 2hrn, trp, tbn, tub	MD	EBM
* Stravinsky, Igor	*Octet for Wind Instruments* fl, cl, 2 bsn, 2 trp, 2 tbn	D	B&H
	Symphonies of Wind Instruments 3 fl, 2 ob, E hrn, 3 cl, 2 bsn, cbsn, 4 hrn, 3 trp, 3 tbn, tub	D	B&H (Rental)
	Concerto for Piano and Wind Instruments pic, 2 fl, 2 ob, E hrn, 2 cl, 2 bsn, cbsn, 4 trp, 3 tbn, tub, timp, st bass	D	B&H (Rental)
Tomasi, Henri	*Fanfares Liturgiques* 3 trp, 4 hrn, 3 tbn, tub	D	AL
* Varèse, Edgard	*Octandre* fl, cl, ob, bsn, hrn, trp, tbn, st bass	MD	CO
* Vaughan Williams, Ralph	*Scherzo Alla Marcia* (from *Symphony No. 8 in D Minor*) pic, fl, 2 ob, 2 cl, 2 bsn, 2 hrn, 2 trp, 3 tbn	MD	OX
Verrall, John	*A Pastoral Elegy* (for Solo Oboe and Winds) fl, 3 cl, bsn, hrn, trp, 3 tbn, tub	M	ACA
Weill, Kurt	*Little Threepenny Music* 2 fl, 2 cl, alto sax, ten sax, 2 bsn, 2 trp, 1 tbn, tub, timp, banjo, piano	M	BOO

Romantic

Composer	Title	Grade	Publisher
d'Indy, Vincent	*Chanson et Danses*, Op. 50 fl, ob, 2 cl, hrn, 2 bsn	MD	TP
Donizetti, Gaetano	*Sinfonia for Winds* fl, 2 ob, 2 cl, 2 hrn, 2 bsn	M	AB

Composer	Title	Grade	Publisher
Dvořák, Anton	*Serenade in D Minor*, Op. 44 2 ob, 2 cl, 2 bsn, cbsn (opt). 3 hrn, cello, st bass	D	IN
Gounod, Charles	*Petite Symphonie* fl, 2 ob, 2 cl, 2 hrn, 2 bsn	M	EGB
Grieg, Edvard	*Funeral Music* 3 trp, 4 hrn, 3 tbn, bar, tub, 2 perc	MD	KING
Sibelius, Jan	*Suite for Band* (1891) cl, 2 cor, 2 hrn, bar, tub	M	WIND
Spohr, Louis	*Notturno for Turkish Band,* Op. 34 fl (pic), 2 ob, 2 cl, 2 bsn, cbsn, 2 hrn, 2 trp, post horn (cornet), tbn, 2 perc	M	AB
* Strauss, Richard	*Serenade in Eb*, Op. 7 2 fl, 2 ob, 2 cl, 4 hrn, 2 bsn, cbsn (tub)	MD	IN
	Suite in Bb, Op. 4 2 fl, 2 ob, 2 cl, 4 hrn, 2 bsn, cbsn	MD	WIND
	Sonatina (Symphony) in Eb ("Cheerful Workshop") 2 fl, 2 ob, 4 cl, bass cl, 4 hrn, 2 bsn, cbsn	D	B&H (Rental)
	Sonatina (Symphony) in F ("From an Invalid's Workshop") 2 fl, 2 ob, 4 cl, bass cl, 4 hrn, 2 bsn, cbsn	D	B&H
Weber, Carl Maria von	*March* (1826) fl, 2 ob, 2 cl, 2 bsn, 2 hrn, 2 trp, tbn	M	MR

Classical

Composer	Title	Grade	Publisher
* Beethoven, Ludwig van	*Five Short Pieces for Wind Ensemble* pic, 2 fl, 2 ob, 2 cl, 2 bsn, cbsn, 2 trp, 2 hrn, perc	M	GS
	Octet in Eb, Op. 103 2 ob, 2 cl, 2 hrn, 2 bsn	MD	CFP
	Rondino in Eb, Op. Posthumous 2 ob, 2 cl, 2 hrn, 2 bsn	MD	IN

Composer	Title	Grade	Publisher
	Sextet in Eb, Op. 71 2 cl, 2 hrn, 2 bsn	MD	IN
* Haydn, Franz Joseph	*Divertimento No. 1 in Bb* (Chorale St. Antoni) 2 ob, 3 bsn, cbsn (st bass), 2 hrn	M	CFP
	Octet in F Major 2 ob, 2 cl, 2 hrn, 2 bsn	M	IN
	Three English Marches 2 cl, 2 bsn, serpent (bsn/tbn), 2 hrn, trp, perc (opt)	M	MR
	Feldpartie in C 2 ob, 2 hrn, 2 bsn	M	MR
	Divertimento in F 2 ob, 2 hrn, 2bsn	M	MR
	March in G 2 ob, 2 hrn, 2 bsn	M	MR
* Mozart, Wolfgang A.	*Divertimento in Eb*, K. 166 2 ob, 2 cl, 2 E hrn, 2 hrn, 2 bsn	MD	AMP
	Divertimento in Eb, K. 196e 2 ob, 2 cl, 2 hrn, 2 bsn	M	MR
	Serenade in Bb, K. 196f 2 cl, 2 hrn, 2 bsn	MD	BM
	Serenade No. 10 (Gran Partita), K. 361 2 ob, 4 cl, 4 hrn, 2 bsn, cbsn (tub)	D	KAL
	Serenade No. 11 in Eb, K. 375 2 ob, 2 cl, 2 hrn, 2 bsn	MD	MR
	Serenade No. 12 in C Minor, K. 388 2 ob, 2 cl, 2 hrn, 2 bsn	D	MR
	Serenade, K. 388 2 ob, 2 cl, 2 hrn, 2 bsn	M	MR

Renaissance-Baroque

Composer	Title	Grade	Publisher
Bach, J. Christian	*Six Wind Sinfonias* 2 cl, 2 hrn, 2 bsn	MD	EBM

Composer	Title	Grade	Publisher
Bach, C. P. E.	*Six Sonatas* 2 fl, 2 cl, 2 hrn, bsn	M	MR
Bonelli, Aurelio	*Toccata* (Athalanta) Antiphonal Brass: Ch I: trp, hrn (trp), tbn (hrn), bar (tbn), tub (opt) Ch II: (same)	M	KING
* Gabrieli, Giovanni	*Canzon Duodecimi toni* (from *Sacre Symphoniae*, 1597) Antiphonal Brass: Ch I: 2 trp, hrn (trp), 2 tbn (bar) Ch II: 2 trp, hrn (trp), 2 tbn, tub	MD	KING
	Canzon noni toni Antiphonal Brass: Ch I: 2 trp, hrn (tbn), bar (tub) Ch II: (same)	MD	KING
	Canzon septimi toni No. 1 Antiphonal Brass: Ch I: trp, hrn (trp), tbn, bar (tub) Ch II: (same)	MD	MER
	Sonata octavi toni Antiphonal Brass: Ch I: 2 trp, hrn (tbn), bar, tub Ch II: (same)	MD	KING
	Sonata pian e forte Antiphonal Brass: Ch I: 2 trp, hrn, tbn Ch II: hrn, 3 tbn	MD	KING
	Canzoni 27 and 28 (1608) Antiphonal Brass: Ch I: 2 trp, 2 tbn Ch II: 2 trp, 2 tbn	MD	MR
Handel, George F.	*Music for the Royal Fireworks* 3 ob (3 cl), 2 bsn, cbsn, 3 hrn, 3 trp in C, timp, 3 trp in B♭ (ad lib), 3 tbn (ad lib), strings (optional)	MD	OX
	Water Music 3 fl (alto fl), 3 ob (E hrn), 5 bsn (cbsn), 2 hrn, 3 trp, timp	M	CFP (Rental)

Key to Publishers

AB	Alexander Broude, Inc. 225 West 57th Street New York City 10019		EA	European American Retail Music P.O. Box 850 Valley Forge, Pennsylvania
AL	Alphonse Leduc Éditions Musicales 175 Rue St-Honofe Paris, France		EBM	Edward B. Marks Music Corp. c/o Belwin-Mills Publishing Corp. 25 Deshon Drive Melville, New York 11746
ACA	American Composers Alliance 170 West 74th Street New York City 10023		ED	Editions Durand & Cie 4 Place de la Madeleine Paris, France (Theodore Presser, Sole Agent)
AMP	Associated Music Publishers, Inc. 866 Third Avenue New York City 10022		EGB	Editions G. Billaudot 14, Rue de l'Echiquier Paris, France
B&H	Boosey and Hawkes, Inc. 200 Smith Street Farmingdale, New York 11735		EV	Elkan-Vogel, Inc. Presser Place Bryn Mawr, Pennsylvania 10910
BM	Belwin-Mills Publishing Corp. 25 Deshon Drive Melville, New York 11746		FITZ	H. T. FitzSimons 615 N. LaSalle Street Chicago, Illlinois 60610
BOO	Joseph Boonin, Inc. P.O. Box 2124 South Hackensack, New Jersey 07606		GS	G. Schirmer, Inc. 866 Third Avenue New York City 10022
CFP	C. F. Peters Corp. 373 Park Avenue South New York City 10016		GM	Galaxy Music Corp. c/o E. C. Schirmer Music Company 112 South Street Boston, Massachusetts
CHAP	Chappell & Company, Inc. 810 Seventh Avenue New York City 10019		HM	Highland Music Company 1311 North Highland Ave. Hollywood, California 90028
CO	Colfranc Music Publishing Corp. c/o Belwin-Mills Publishing Corp. 25 Deshon Drive Melville, New York 11746		IN	International Music Company 509 Fifth Avenue New York City
COL	Franco Colombo, Inc. c/o Belwin-Mills Publishing Corp. 25 Deshon Drive Melville, New York 11746		KAL	Edwin F. Kalmus Music Publishers Miami Dade Industrial Park P.O. Box 1007 Opa Locka, Florida 33054

KING Robert King Music Company
112 A Main Street
North Easton, Massachusetts 02356

LEE Leeds Music Corporation
c/o Belwin-Mills Publishing Corp.
25 Deshon Drive
Melville, New York 11746

LM Ludwig Music Publishing Co.
557-67 East 140th St.
Cleveland, Ohio 44110

MCA Music Corporation of America
c/o Belwin-Mills Publishing Corp.
25 Deshon Drive
Melville, New York 11746

MER Mercury Music Corporation
Presser Place
Bryn Mawr, Pennsylvania 19010

MILL Mills Music, Inc.
Division of Belwin-Mills
25 Deshon Drive
Melville, New York 11746

MM Merion Music Inc.
Theodore Presser Co.
Presser Place
Bryn Mawr, Pennsylvania 19010

MR Musica Rara
c/o Magnamusic Distributors Inc.
Sharon, Connecticut 06069

OX Oxford University Press
200 Madison Avenue
New York City 10016

PIC Peer International Corp.
c/o Southern Music Publishing Company
1740 Broadway
New York City 10019

PM Piedmont Music Company, Inc.
c/o Marks Music Corp.
25 Deshon Drive
Melville, New York 11746

RM Rochester Music Publisher, Inc.
358 Aldrich Road
Fairport, New York 14450

SF Sam Fox Publishing Co., Inc.
170 N. E. 33rd Street
Ft. Lauderdale, Florida 33307

SHAW Shawnee Press, Inc.
Delaware Water Gap
Pennsylvania 18327

STAFF Staff Music Publishing Company
c/o Plymouth Music
170 N. E. 33rd Street
Ft. Lauderdale, Florida 33307

TP Theodore Presser Company
Presser Place
Bryn Mawr, Pennsylvania 19010

WEIN Weintraub Music Company
33 West 60th Street
New York City 10023

WIM Western International Music Inc.
2859 Holt Avenue
Los Angeles 90034

WIND Wind Instrument's New Dawn Society
(W.I.N.D.S.)
P.O. Box 513
Northridge, California 91324